Diabetic Meals In 30 Minutes—Or Less!

Diabetic Meals In 30 Minutes—Or Less!

Robyn Webb

American
Diabetes
Association®

Book Acquisitions
Susan Reynolds

Book Editor
Laurie Guffey

Page design and typesetting services by
Insight Graphics

Cover design by
Contemporary Books, Inc.

Cover photograph by
Chris Cassidy

Food styling by
Jenny Thornton

Illustrations by
Rebecca Grace Jones

Nutritional analyses by
Nutritional Computing Concepts, Inc.

Printed in the United States of America

American Diabetes Association
1701 N. Beauregard Street
Alexandria, VA 22311

Library of Congress Cataloging-in-Publication Data

Webb, Robyn.
Diabetic meals in 30 minutes—or less! / Robyn Webb.
p. cm.
Includes bibliographical references and index.
ISBN 0-945448-60-0 (pbk.)
1. Diabetes—Diet therapy—Recipes.   I. Title.
RC662.W355 1996
641.5'6314—dc20   96-13157   CIP

*This book is lovingly dedicated to my mother
Ruth, whose own challenges inspire me
and others around her every day.*

Contents

Foreword...ix
Preface...xi
Acknowledgments...xiii
Introduction...1
  How This Book Will Save You Time...1
  Organization 101: Dozens of Tips for Every Cook
    To Get Food on the Table in a Flash!....................................2
  What's in the Cupboard: Quick Fixes.....................................11
  25 Recipe Ideas For:
    Beans...11
    Broth...12
    Pasta...13
    Rice...15
    Fish..16
Appealing Appetizers..17
Soup's On!...29
Super Salads...41
Vegetarian Fare..55
The Daily Catch..69
Perfect Poultry...81
Lean Beef and Pork..101
Very Quick Vegetables..113
Sweet Endings..127
Complete Menus for Every Day and Entertaining.................137
  Romantic Dining...138
  Lazy Sunday Brunch...143
  Country French Dinner..148
  Warm Summer Evening..153
  Dinner Italiano..158
Appendix...165
Index..169

Foreword

Eating healthy, tasty foods is an important part of successful, lifelong diabetes management. We've learned that people with diabetes can choose from a wider variety of delicious foods than we once thought. The American Diabetes Association Nutrition Recommendations stress an individualized approach to self-management, based on your personal lifestyle and diabetes management goals. Today there is no single, recommended "ADA" diet. Instead, we're delighted to offer you this collection of easy-to-prepare, low-fat recipes to help you broaden your individual mealtime choices. Improving your food choices leads to better health, and that means better diabetes management.

Diabetic Meals In 30 Minutes—Or Less! supports our goal of improving overall health through optimal nutrition. All recipes in this book are accompanied by nutritional analyses so you can be fully informed about what you're eating. The starch, fruit, and milk exchanges can be interchanged to accommodate your individual meal plan. For people who have normal fat levels in their blood and maintain a reasonable weight, we recommend that 30% of daily calories come from fat (with only 10% from saturated fats). This book will help you find delicious ways to stay within those guidelines.

We used to think that people with diabetes needed to avoid simple sugars like sucrose, and eat more complex carbohydrates like rice and potatoes. We now know there's no evidence that including sugar as part of your meal plan will hurt your blood glucose control. However, you must be careful to substitute simple sugars in your total meal plan, and not just add them to your other carbohydrates. This means you now have greater freedom when making your healthy food choices, and don't need to feel as "deprived" or different as you may have before.

With that in mind, we're happy to share this cookbook, packed full of interesting, flavorful ways to improve your meals—and your health.

Frank Vinicor, MD, MPH
President, American Diabetes Association

Preface

Automatic teller machines, express check-out aisles at the supermarket, one-hour photo shops, overnight mail—what do all of these things have in common? All are designed to provide quick service to busy consumers. In today's world, we all want to know how we can do things faster, better, and more efficiently. And when it comes to home cooking, we want tasty, nutritious food that doesn't take forever to cook.

How can busy people satisfy their need for healthy, delicious meals and still have some time left over to enjoy life? Enter this book. *Diabetic Meals In 30 Minutes—Or Less!* is more than just a cookbook—it is your tool for complete kitchen success.

Preparing foods faster also includes having an organized kitchen. In the first chapter of this book, you'll find dozens of tips on how to get organized now. You will learn how to plan better, shop smarter, and arrange your kitchen in the most efficient way possible.

Imagine opening your kitchen cupboard at the end of a long day and knowing all the dinner fixings you need are right there. The second chapter reveals five staple items no home should be without, and provides 25 ideas for quick meals you can make in a flash.

Learn how to cook low-fat, high-fiber, healthy delicious food, with the over 100 mouthwatering recipes included here. You'll master exciting dishes like Turkey Provençal, Bombay Chicken, or Indian Rice Curry and have them on the table in 30 minutes or less. With these recipes you'll never be bored—and you won't have time to get tired of cooking.

And for those special occasions, you'll find five fabulous menus, complete with shopping lists, recipes, and a timetable for the food preparation steps, so your meal is ready when you are!

Turn your kitchen into a cooking metropolis. Have fun in the kitchen, with guaranteed delicious results!

Acknowledgments

Many heartfelt thanks go to these people behind the scenes, for without their support this book would not have become a reality. I appreciate the expertise of Susan Reynolds and Laurie Guffey of the American Diabetes Association, who coordinated the development and editing of this book professionally and with ease. I thank them for their partnership and their belief that this book was needed and wanted. My gratitude to Lyn Wheeler, whose detailed perfection in analyzing the recipes can be matched by no other professional. I could not do without her valuable suggestions and thoughts. My staff, Austin Zackari and Kathy Chamberlain, supplied many great ideas and took countless trips to the grocery store. My husband, Allan, provided love, support, and patience—even when I was cooking for everyone else but him! Finally, thanks to all my cooking school students, for their helpful input and their commitment to healthy living.

Introduction

How This Book Will Save You Time

Imagine your day as a clock. Do you spend too much of your valuable time on food preparation? Or are you unable to squeeze out any time to prepare nutritious meals without relying on unhealthy and boring prepackaged food? This book will show you how to create wonderful meals without sacrificing precious time for the other things you need to do. Following are some tips that will help you make the best use of this book.

Preparation times are given for each recipe. This is the time it takes to prepare the ingredients for the recipe, but marinating time and cooking time are not included. Most of these recipes have very short cooking times, however. Marinating is a great technique to use because it adds so much flavor to meats, and you can marinate a meal overnight, thus shortening the actual preparation and cooking time. The goal of this book is to save time, but also to help you prepare interesting, good-tasting food with great flavor.

To help you improve efficiency in the kitchen, the following section outlines dozens of organization tips. You may find, with practice, that your own preparation times may be shorter than those listed here!

Every effort has been made to assure a quality product. Therefore, the recipes often call for fresh ingredients (especially fruits, vegetables, and herbs), and only include prepackaged food products when their use is necessary and does not affect the recipe's flavor. By practicing the timesaving skills presented here, you will find that using fresh ingredients does not add substantially to the recipe preparation times.

Low-calorie margarine and artificial sweeteners are used very rarely. When low-calorie margarine is used, it is to assure the texture of the product. Try to use monounsaturated fats like canola or olive oil instead of low-calorie margarine, which can be high in a substance called trans-fatty acids.

To keep the fat content down, but great flavor in, most of the vegetables are sauteed in small amounts of olive oil. Use a nonstick skillet so the food doesn't burn. If necessary, add a little broth or wine to prevent any burning (not included in nutrient analyses). Using a nonstick skillet helps save time in clean-up, too.

Remember, food was meant to be enjoyed and savored! You'll find that these recipes will soon become a valuable part of your healthy, and satisfying, meal plan. Bon Appetit!

Organization 101

Cooking quickly does not mean night after night of tasteless, high-fat, prepackaged foods. Getting organized from the planning stage through the actual food preparation and clean-up will save you many hours of wasted time! Here's how.

Meal Planning

Cooking several days' worth of meals involves planning ahead. Decide before you go to the grocery store what you want to cook, and you'll avoid those pesky repeat trips for a few forgotten items. A well-thought-out plan saves you time and money.

Start by looking through this book and decide what recipes you would like to prepare for the week. Plan to make enough for lunch leftovers. You can prepare some of the meat and fish recipes for dinner, then combine the leftovers with salad fixings for a quick lunch. Or, prepare 5 or 6 dinners and plan to have leftovers 1–2 nights a week. This saves you from having to prepare 7 different dinners each week.

Prepare your plan on paper, or, if you are computer savvy, prepare a weekly menu plan to store and retrieve whenever you need to. Try to avoid relying on your memory to create a menu plan. You'll be more organized and efficient if you put it in writing.

Prepare your shopping list from your plan. Organize the list like the layout of your grocery store, usually starting with the produce department. Work your way around the perimeter of the store first, then go down the aisles. Most of the food you should be shopping for will be located on the perimeter of the store anyway, since this is where the fresh food is stocked.

About once a month, shop for staples. You will save lots of time during your weekly trips if the bulk of your dry goods is already stocked in your home. You may want to think a little like a restaurant manager does, and always buy a standard quantity of the staples you seem to go through quickly so you are never caught short. For example, your standard quantity for onions may be one prepackaged bag, since you will probably use onions in many recipes and they keep well in your pantry. Look to see what staples you go through quickly and establish a personal standard quantity for them.

Try to shop on the same day each week if you can. That way, efficient weekly shopping will become part of your normal routine, rather than several frantic, last-minute affairs.

Although it is tempting to shop for bargains, think twice about driving to more than 3 or 4 stores to find them. The cost of your time and gas may not be worth the savings in the bargain you find. But, of course, look for the best quality food possible.

As you plan your menus, check to see what you already have in the refrigerator, freezer, and pantry. Many people are surprised to find what is already stocked in their kitchens. See the **Quick Fixes** section for ideas of meals to prepare from kitchen staples, p. 11.

When planning a meal, try not to rely on recipes that call for too many pieces of kitchen equipment that you have to clean later. Also, if you are preparing casserole-type meals in which everything is mixed together, mix your ingredients right in the casserole dish you plan to use to bake the meal. Clean-up will go much quicker.

A few times a week, rely on recipes for one-pot meals. You'll get all your vegetables, protein, and starch in one pot, making for easy meal planning, shopping time, and clean-up.

When planning an entire meal, select recipes that don't all require the oven or stove. You may run out of room, or waste time waiting for one part of the meal to finish baking before the other part can go in the oven. If you can, cook some of the meal in advance, so you're not in a last-minute panic trying to get out all of the food served at the right temperature and the right time.

Trying new recipes and using new ingredients is fun and adventurous. But you'll save time relying on and stocking familiar ingredients you know you'll use time and time again. Going out of your way to purchase an exotic ingredient and not being able to use that ingredient again may not be worth the trouble.

Kitchen Organization

Inefficiency in the kitchen stops many people from preparing delicious, fresh meals. A kitchen that is easy to work in will be more pleasurable and save you time, too. Here are some ways to get organized now.

Take a little time to review all your kitchen equipment. Just like cleaning out your clothes closet, if an item hasn't been used in years or is damaged, toss it. You won't miss it if you never use it. Make a written list of all the kitchen equipment you are saving.

Look carefully at your preferred cooking style and how often you need to prepare meals. For example, if you're cooking for one, it might be easier for you to just chop a few vegetables by hand, rather than lugging out the big food processor for just one or two ingredients.

Get rid of equipment that is used to make unhealthy food, such as fondue pots and deep-fat fryers. Even if these items are precious wedding gifts, at best they will only collect dust in your cupboard, and at worst you'll be making high-fat mistakes with them. Your body will thank you!

Put like items together. Nothing slows your cooking time down more than hunting for an item, only to find it in some obscure place. Store seldom-used items in your basement or closet, away from items you use every day.

If you have kitchen counter space, place frequently used condiments, grains, and pastas in pretty containers right on or near the counter where you prepare your food. It's quicker to reach for them there than dig through several cabinets. If you do not have spare counter space, but extra kitchen space, consider purchasing a small rolling cart on which to put these frequently used items. You will also know much quicker when you need to replenish your stock!

Your knives should never be placed in a drawer—this ruins their sharpness. Store them in a wooden block or hang a magnetic strip made for hanging knives (most kitchen shops sell them) on the backsplash of your kitchen wall. Place the knives upright onto the strip for easy access.

What to Buy

These items will make your culinary life more pleasant!

Buy the best knives you can afford. A well-made carbon steel knife is invaluable, no matter how frequently you cook. Food is much easier to prepare with a high-quality set of knives. Consider purchasing at a minimum an 8- or 10-inch chef's knife for most of your chopping, a paring knife for smaller foods, and a good bread knife.

Purchase at least one nonstick skillet. They save you time in clean-up, and are more healthful to cook with.

A pasta pot with a steamer/colander insert is a wonderful way to drain pasta without the chore of lifting the pasta to drain in the sink. The steamer insert can also be used to cook vegetables and fish.

A wok is the most versatile piece of kitchen equipment you can invest in. Besides quick stir-frying, a wok is useful for steaming foods (place a rack inside), and if it is deep enough, can even be used for making soup. A nonstick wok will save you clean-up time.

A food processor is useful for big jobs of slicing and shredding. However, make sure you have room to store one. Be prepared to clean your food processor every time you use it. Consider starting with a smaller version to see how often you really use it. Avoid using a food processor for chopping vegetables with a high water content, such as onions. One second too long, and you'll have onion soup!

Meal Preparation

The time you'll save in the kitchen is time you can devote to other healthy pursuits, like exercising or being with family and friends. Even if you enjoy the time you spend cooking, these tips will add to your culinary efficiency and overall pleasure.

Easy Ways to Prepare Vegetables

Healthy food is often flavored with onion and garlic. These two ingredients replace much of the flavor removed with excess fat and sodium. Here are some easy ways to work with them.

To chop onions with ease, first slice the onion in two pieces lengthwise, keeping the root end on. Then peel the skin on each half, again keeping the root end on. Make three vertical slices without cutting through the end. Then make several horizontal slices, without cutting through the end. Then turn the onion, and proceed to slice downward. You will have uniformly diced onions, and a minimum of onion tears!

To prepare flavorful garlic, chop it by hand rather than using a garlic press. Lay the garlic clove on a working surface and place the flat side of a large knife blade against it. Carefully smack the blade with your fist. This flattens the garlic and makes the skin easy to remove. Make a few cuts with the knife vertically, and then chop.

After you have chopped onions and garlic, you can freeze them for future use. Just spread the chopped vegetables onto a small, nonstick cookie sheet. Spreading them out prevents them from clumping together in a ball when frozen. Cover with plastic wrap and place the sheet in the freezer for two hours. When frozen, scrape the onions and garlic into plastic freezer bags. Put about 1/2 to 1 cup at a time in a bag. When recipes call for cooking onions or garlic, just remove your pre-chopped frozen vegetable from the freezer and begin to cook. Add an additional 2–3 minutes to cooking time. This technique is a real time-saver! For fresh salads and cold foods, it is best to use fresh onions and garlic.

Slicing mushrooms is easy with an egg slicer. Just stem the mushrooms and place them in the slicer for even slices.

Snip herbs with a pair of scissors right into the pot. Use the stems of the herbs, except for tough stems like those on rosemary and sage.

Prepare vegetables one day ahead of time and place them in plastic bags to save time. Try to do this only one day in advance. Longer than that, and the vegetables will begin to lose their vitamin content and freshness.

If you are preparing several recipes together, read through all of them first. If the recipes have similar ingredients that need to be chopped or sliced, do all of the same vegetable first.

When you bring salad greens home, wash them first in a salad spinner to remove any dirt, then place the greens in a plastic bag wrapped with damp paper towels. They will stay fresh for an extra day.

Most marinades and salad dressing can be made in advance. Most of the marinades and dressings in this book will keep in a refrigerated screw-top jar for 1–3 days prior to preparing the rest of the recipe.

Prepare rice, especially long-cooking brown rice, in advance (for tips, see **Vegetarian Fare**, p. 55).

Time-Saving Tips

Always, always read the recipe through at least once before beginning to use it! You might find an ingredient that needs to marinate overnight. Choose another recipe for tonight's dinner, and enjoy the marinated meat tomorrow!

Learn to dovetail when you cook. No, it's not the latest dance step, but an efficient way to make use of your time! While a sauce is simmering or a food is marinating, be busy preparing the next step in the recipe or go on to the next recipe. You will find out more about how to dovetail in the **Complete Menus** section of this book (p. 137).

Just like you set aside time to go grocery shopping each week, set aside a window of time to regularly cook each day. We are an appointment-oriented society, so make a "date" with yourself to prepare healthy meals. Make cooking fun by putting on great music to listen to, or by sharing the cooking tasks with family members or friends. Have children help too. Three-year-olds can place cut vegetables in a bag and mix ingredients together. If it's too distracting or unsafe having small children around in the kitchen, plan on cooking when children are otherwise occupied.

Consider freezing leftovers for later use. Soups, stews, and other casserole dishes freeze well. Line casserole dishes with foil, place the casserole inside, and freeze. Once the food is frozen, lift it out of the dish by its foil edges, wrap with more foil, and return to the freezer. Then wash your dish and store it.

Make sure your work surface is free of clutter, such as papers, used dishes, and toys. Keep the kitchen ready for food preparation.

Make sure the lighting in your kitchen is good. Poor lighting will slow down your cooking time. Think about adding some under-cabinet lighting if you do a lot of work on kitchen counters.

Basic Storage Techniques

Proper storage is as important as food preparation. What a waste of time if the food you prepare is improperly stored and goes bad! First, make sure your refrigerator and freezer are at the proper temperatures: 40 degrees F or less for the refrigerator and 0 degrees F or less for the freezer.

Leftover chicken broth can be frozen for future use in ice cube trays. When recipes call for broth, just pop out a cube (about 1 Tbsp each).

Herbs can also be frozen like broth. Just snip the leftover herb into the trays, cover each cube with water, and freeze. When recipes call for an herb in a hot dish, pop out the cube and add to the dish.

Eggs should be left in their original cartons and stored in the back of your refrigerator for best freshness.

Use chicken within 48 hours and fish within 24 hours for best freshness.

Consider storing flours in the refrigerator or freezer. Whole-grain flours will keep better in the refrigerator or freezer (this prevents them from becoming rancid).

Are You A Pack Rat?

My dried herbs and spices are more than one year old.
My baking powder and baking soda are more than one year old.
My dried pastas and grains are more than one year old.
My frozen chicken is more than 8 months old.
My frozen fish is more than 6 months old.
My flour is more than 8 months old.

If you answered "yes" to these questions, get out the tissues, wipe your tears, grab a trash bag, and start tossing!

To be most efficient in the kitchen—and produce the best-tasting food—try not to keep staples past their prime.

☞ When purchasing dried herbs and spices, buy the smallest quantity available. When storing bottles, place them where you can see them. That way, you can avoid wasting time hunting around in a crowded cupboard. At kitchen shops, buy raised platforms for spices to make them more visible. Some spice racks fit in a kitchen drawer, so you can arrange your spices in rows and find them easily. Lazy susans are sometimes difficult to use, because spices fall off them and bottles can hide behind each other.

☞ Keep your baking powder and baking soda no more than one year. Longer than that, and their leavening power begins to fade.

☞ Pastas and grains should also be used within one year. If your pasta has little white specks on it, it's too old! To keep them fresh, store pastas and grains in tightly sealed glass containers.

☞ Use frozen chicken within 8 months, and fish within 6 months—sooner than that if you can. Frozen meat and fish will never taste quite as good as fresh.

☞ Flours, like other grains, should be stored in glass containers. Whole-grain flours, such as whole-wheat flour, should always be kept in the refrigerator. If left at room temperature, whole-grain flours will become rancid due to their bran and germ content. You can even store flour in the freezer without affecting its flavor.

Quality Clean-Up

All your efforts to seek out time-saving recipes will be for naught if it takes you hours to wash 50 different pots and pans. Let's clean up, efficiently!

⌀ Consider using the same dish for mixing and baking.

⌀ Clean as you go!

⌀ If you are preparing pasta and vegetables, place the pasta in the pot first. Add the vegetables 3–4 minutes before cooking time is up. You'll end up with crisp vegetables and only one pot to wash.

⌀ When grilling, coat the rack with oil or spray. It will be much easier to clean. When cooking puddings or other sticky foods, also coat the saucepan with spray to prevent sticking and messy clean-up.

🪥 Keep a small toothbrush next to the sink for hard-to-clean nooks and crannies on graters and strainers.

What's in the Cupboard: Quick Fixes

Many cookbooks will give you a list of items to stock in the pantry, but how do you make a meal from them? The next time you think there's nothing to eat at home, look again! Select one of the following 25 ideas and use staples you already have—a meal is just moments away. See **Appendix** (p. 165) for all nutrient analyses.

Canned Beans

Beans are not only nutritious, they add interest to any dish and are easy to prepare. Using canned beans is perfectly acceptable—just rinse them for several minutes under cold running water to get rid of the excess salt. Be sure the beans have no sugar added. You can also freeze cooked beans in a plastic container or freezer bag. Just add cooked frozen beans to a stew or soup and cook a little longer.

Quick Idea #1: *Salsa Salad.* Take one 15-oz can drained and rinsed black beans; 2 Tbsp salsa; 1 cup frozen, thawed corn kernels; 1 cup fresh or frozen and thawed carrot slices; 2 Tbsp lime juice; and 1 garlic clove, minced. Combine together and serve. Makes 6 servings.

Quick Idea #2: *Bean Spread.* Puree one 15-oz can drained and rinsed kidney or pinto beans with 1 cup low-fat ricotta cheese, 1 tsp ground cumin, 2 tsp chili powder, and 3 Tbsp canned salsa. Puree until smooth. Use as a dip or as a sandwich filling. Makes 16 servings, 2 Tbsp each.

Quick Idea #3: *Zippy Pasta.* Take any 15-oz can of beans, drained and rinsed, and combine it with 6 cups cooked pasta. Add 1/2 cup rehydrated dried mushrooms. Add 1/2 cup low-calorie Italian salad dressing and chill. Makes 6 servings.

Quick Idea #4: *Navy Bean Soup.* Take 1 15-oz can drained and rinsed navy beans and combine with 1 28-oz can crushed tomatoes; 1 10-oz can low-fat, low-sodium chicken broth; 1 cup fresh, sliced, or frozen and thawed zucchini; 1 cup fresh, sliced, or frozen and thawed carrots; 1 tsp each basil and oregano; and 1 cup cooked pasta shells. Heat in a stockpot for 2–3 minutes. Makes 6 servings.

Quick Idea #5: *Quick Refried Beans.* In a skillet over medium-high heat, heat 1 Tbsp olive oil. Add 1 medium chopped onion. Saute for 5 minutes. Add 2 Tbsp chili powder. Cook for 1 minute. Add 1 15-oz can drained and rinsed kidney beans. Mash the beans with a potato masher. Raise the heat to high and cook for 1–2 minutes until beans are a little dry. Makes 6 servings, 1/4 cup each.

Canned Broth

Although it is nice to prepare fresh broth, you won't always have the time. When buying canned broth, look for a low-fat, low-sodium variety. Check bouillon cubes for high fat and high sodium content before using them.

Quick Idea #1: *Turkey Ball Soup.* Heat 3 cups low-fat, low-sodium chicken broth. Take 1 lb ground turkey breast meat (your butcher will do this for you) and combine it with 1 egg, 3 Tbsp dry breadcrumbs, 1 Tbsp Worcestershire sauce, and fresh ground pepper and salt to taste. Roll into 1-inch meatballs. Drop into boiling broth and cook until turkey is cooked through, about 10 minutes. Add 1 cup leftover cooked rice or pasta. Cook 1 more minute. Makes 6 servings.

Quick Idea #2: *Clear Asian Soup.* Boil 3 cups low-fat, low-sodium chicken broth. Add 2 carrots, sliced; 1 celery stalk, sliced; 1 tsp ginger; 1 Tbsp chopped scallions; 2 Tbsp lite soy sauce; 1 Tbsp sherry; and 3 cups cooked pasta. Cook for 10 minutes and enjoy a delicious, quick soup. Makes 6 servings.

Quick Idea #3: *Rice and Pea Soup.* Boil 4 cups low-fat, low-sodium chicken broth. Add 3 cups cooked leftover brown rice, half of a 10-oz package of frozen peas, and 1 sprig of rosemary. Cook for 5 minutes. Sprinkle with 1 Tbsp grated Parmesan cheese for a comforting soup without fuss. Makes 6 servings.

Quick Idea #4: *Tasty Pasta Soup.* Take 3 cups leftover cooked pasta and add it to 4 cups low-fat, low-sodium chicken broth. Bring to a boil. Add 1 cup leftover cooked, diced chicken and 1/2 cup canned diced tomatoes. Cook for 5 minutes. Makes 6 servings.

Quick Idea #5: *Fast Onion Soup.* Heat 1 Tbsp olive oil in a skillet over medium-high heat. Add 3 cups sliced onions. Saute for 10 minutes until onions are soft. Add the onions to 6 cups boiling low-fat, low-sodium chicken broth. Add 2 Tbsp dry white wine. Grind in pepper. Serve over toasted bread slices in individual bowls. Makes 6 servings.

Pasta

Everyone loves pasta. There are so many varieties from which to choose, you'll never become bored. In addition to the wonderful recipes in this book, here are some fast ideas to combine pasta with other items from your cupboard and refrigerator. Pasta can be prepared and kept in an airtight container for 1 week.

Quick Idea #1: *Pasta Pie.* To 6 cups cooked spaghetti, add 1 beaten egg white, 1 Tbsp olive oil, 1 Tbsp grated Parmesan cheese, and 2 tsp dried oregano. Combine well. Place in a 9-inch glass pie plate. Bake for 15 minutes until pasta is slightly browned. Fill the center with 2 cups cooked vegetables. Makes 6 servings.

Quick Idea #2: *Artichoke Pasta Salad.* Combine 6 cups cooked, cooled, small shell pasta with 1 14-oz can water-packed artichoke hearts; 1/2 package frozen, thawed peas; 10 rehydrated, sun-dried tomatoes; and 1/2 cup low-fat salad dressing. Toss well and serve on lettuce. Makes 6 servings.

Quick Idea #3: *Sesame Noodles.* During the last 3 minutes of cooking 6 cups of fettucine noodles, add 1 10-oz package of mixed vegetables (vegetables with corn, peas, or additional pasta are not included in nutrient analysis). Drain pasta and vegetables. Add 2 tsp sesame oil, 2 Tbsp toasted sesame seeds, and 1/4 cup sliced scallions. Makes 6 servings.

Quick Idea #4: *Hungarian Noodles.* To 6 cups cooked wide noodles, add 1 cup sliced cabbage to the water 3 minutes before cooking time is up. Drain. Add in 1 cup frozen, thawed carrots. In a large saucepan, add the cooked noodles, cabbage, and carrots. Add in 1 cup low-fat sour cream and 1 tsp caraway seeds. Grind in fresh pepper. Cook 1 minute. Makes 6 servings.

Quick Idea #5: *Fast Mediterranean Meal.* Add 1 15-oz can drained chickpeas to 6 cups cooked small elbow macaroni. Drizzle in 2 Tbsp balsamic vinegar and 2 tsp olive oil. Sprinkle with 1 Tbsp grated Parmesan cheese. Serve at room temperature. Makes 6 servings.

Rice

Rice deserves a little jazzing up—try these ideas. To store uncooked rice, keep it in airtight containers in the refrigerator or a cool pantry. Try different kinds of rice for a flavor change. To prepare brown rice, follow the directions on p. 57. Brown rice does take longer to prepare, but you can prepare it ahead of time and freeze it for later use. For these recipes, use cooked, leftover rice you have in the refrigerator.

Quick Idea #1: *Cool Salad.* Combine 3 cups cooked white or brown rice with 1 cup halved red grapes; 1 Granny Smith apple, diced; 1 Tbsp toasted walnuts; and 1 cup low-fat sour cream. Makes 6 servings.

Quick Idea #2: *Viva Mexicana.* Saute 1 medium onion in 1 Tbsp olive oil for 4 minutes. Add in 2 tsp chili powder and 3 cups cooked brown or white rice. Add in 1 15-oz can drained kidney beans. Top with canned chilies if desired. Cook 1 minute through. Makes 6 servings.

Quick Idea #3: *Down By the Bay.* Saute 2 garlic cloves in 2 tsp olive oil for 1 minute. Add in 2 tsp dried oregano and 3 cups cooked rice. Saute for 2 minutes. Add in 1 10-oz package frozen chopped spinach, thawed and drained well. Add in 1 7-oz can baby shrimp. Cook 1 minute. Makes 6 servings.

Quick Idea #4: *Fast Fried Rice.* In a wok over medium-high heat, heat 2 tsp peanut oil. Add in 2 garlic cloves, minced, and 2 Tbsp sliced scallions. Stir-fry for 30 seconds. Add in 3 cups cooked white or brown rice. Stir-fry for 2 minutes. Add in 1/4 cup lite soy sauce; half of a 10-oz package frozen peas, thawed; and 1 cup bean sprouts. Stir-fry for 2 minutes. Makes 6 servings.

Quick Idea #5: *Rice Crust Pizza.* Take 3 cups cooked white or brown rice. Add 1 egg, beaten; 2 Tbsp grated Parmesan cheese; and 2 tsp basil. Mix well. Press into a round 12-inch pizza pan. Spread evenly. Bake in a 350-degree preheated oven for 10 minutes. Top with 4 oz lite mozzarella cheese, 1 cup low-fat pizza sauce, 1 cup mushrooms, and 1 cup red or green pepper. Return to the oven and bake until cheese melts. Makes 6 servings.

Canned Fish

In a pinch, canned fish will work well. Buy canned tuna and salmon packed in water. Canned salmon is a particularly good source of calcium, with its edible soft bones. For best results, buy solid white tuna and pink salmon.

Quick Idea #1: *Tuna Pate.* In a blender, puree 1 cup 1% cottage cheese, 2 Tbsp scallions, 1 tsp minced parsley, 2 tsp minced dill, and 2 tsp lite soy sauce. Add 1 7-oz can drained tuna. Blend again until smooth. Spread the tuna pate on sandwiches or serve from a crock with crackers. Makes 6 servings.

Quick Idea #2: *Salmon Nicoise.* Toss together 1 16-oz can pink salmon; 1 10-oz package frozen green beans, thawed and drained; 1 14-oz can artichoke hearts, drained; 1 red pepper, diced; and 1/2 cup low-calorie Italian salad dressing. Toss well and serve. Makes 6 servings.

Quick Idea #3: *Tonnato Sauce.* In a skillet over medium-high heat, heat 2 tsp olive oil. Add 1 medium onion, diced. Saute for 4 minutes. Add 2 cups crushed tomatoes, 2 Tbsp dry red wine, and 2 tsp dried oregano. Bring to a boil. Lower the heat and simmer for 10 minutes. Add 1 7-oz can tuna, drained. Add in 1 Tbsp capers. Serve sauce over cooked pasta (not included in nutrient analysis). Makes 6 servings.

Quick Idea #4: *Couscous Tuna Salad.* Toss 1 7-oz can tuna, drained, with 2 cups rehydrated couscous (start out with 1 cup dry couscous, pour 2 cups boiling water over couscous, and let stand for 5 minutes until water is absorbed); 1/2 cup frozen corn, thawed and drained; 2 Tbsp minced cilantro; 2 Tbsp red wine vinegar; and 1 Tbsp olive oil. Grind in fresh pepper and serve at room temperature. Makes 6 servings.

Quick Idea #5: *Quick Salmon Burgers.* Combine 1 7-oz can salmon, drained, with 1 egg, beaten; 2 Tbsp Dijon mustard; 3 Tbsp dry breadcrumbs; and 2 tsp Tabasco sauce. Form into patties and place in a heated nonstick skillet. Cook for 5–6 minutes each side until browned. Makes 6 servings.

Appealing Appetizers

Traditionally, appetizers are like fat magnets: mini-quiches, wrapped sausages, and sour cream dips all spell disaster for a healthy meal plan!

Fortunately, you can make appetizers that taste good, present attractively, and still provide basic good nutrition. All of the recipes in this chapter can be made in advance, so you can concentrate on your guests when they arrive. Or, enjoy them as great snacks.

To dip into the spreads, consider all kinds of vegetables, toasted pita wedges, low-fat baked tortilla chips, low-fat crackers, or mini rice cakes. Try serving the dips in hollowed-out cabbages, zucchini, or yellow squash; colorful pepper cups; a crusty, hollowed-out, round loaf of bread; or a decorative crock.

Host a healthy appetizer party with these easy and delicious recipes!

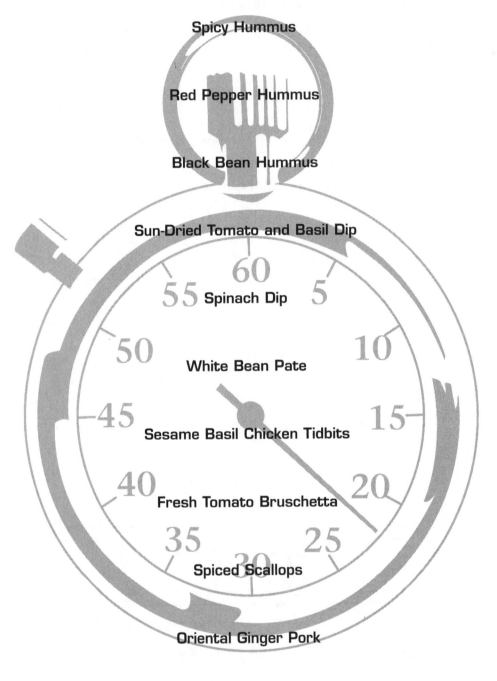

Spicy Hummus

Red Pepper Hummus

Black Bean Hummus

Sun-Dried Tomato and Basil Dip

60

55 Spinach Dip 5

50 10

White Bean Pate

45 15

Sesame Basil Chicken Tidbits

40 20

Fresh Tomato Bruschetta

35 25

30

Spiced Scallops

Oriental Ginger Pork

Spicy Hummus

12 servings/serving size: 2 Tbsp

Everyone likes the Middle Eastern dip called hummus! Made with garbonzo beans (also called chickpeas), hummus is high in fiber and protein. Unfortunately, commercially prepared hummus can be very high in fat, due to the addition of too much sesame tahini (sesame butter) and oil. Here's a lighter version of the traditional dip that you can make yourself.

1 15-oz can chickpeas, drained and rinsed (reserve 1 Tbsp liquid)
1 Tbsp sesame tahini
3 garlic cloves, minced
1 Tbsp lemon juice
1 tsp olive oil
1 tsp cumin
1 tsp coriander
1/2 tsp cayenne pepper
Fresh ground white pepper
2 tsp minced parsley

Starch Exchange	1/2
Calories	48
Total Fat	2 g
Saturated Fat	0 g
Calories from Fat	15
Cholesterol	0 mg
Sodium	34 mg
Total Carbohydrate	7 g
Dietary Fiber	1 g
Sugars	1 g
Protein	2 g

Combine all ingredients in a blender or food processor. Use 1 Tbsp of reserved bean juice to moisten, if necessary. Process until smooth.

Preparation time: 5 minutes

Red Pepper Hummus

12 servings/serving size: 2 Tbsp

This recipe contains sesame tahini, but considerably less than in store-bought hummus.

1/2 cup canned chickpeas, drained
2 roasted red peppers (purchase roasted red peppers in a jar from the condiment aisle in the grocery store)
1 Tbsp sesame tahini
2 Tbsp plain low-fat yogurt
2 garlic cloves, minced
1 Tbsp minced onion
Dash cayenne pepper
Fresh ground pepper to taste

Vegetable Exchange	1
Calories	28
Total Fat	1 g
Saturated Fat	0 g
Calories from Fat	13
Cholesterol	0 mg
Sodium	69 mg
Total Carbohydrate	3 g
Dietary Fiber	1 g
Sugars	2 g
Protein	1 g

Combine the first three ingredients in a blender until smooth. Add the remaining ingredients and process until smooth.

Preparation time: 8 minutes

Black Bean Hummus

12 servings/serving size: 2 Tbsp

Serve this dip with fat-free tortilla chips, pita bread wedges, or raw vegetables.

1 15-oz can black beans, drained
1 Tbsp sesame tahini
1 Tbsp low-fat sour cream
4 garlic cloves, minced
1 Tbsp minced tomato
1 Tbsp lime juice
1 tsp cumin
Fresh ground pepper to taste

Starch Exchange	1/2
Calories	43
Total Fat	1 g
Saturated Fat	0 g
Calories from Fat	8
Cholesterol	0 mg
Sodium	45 mg
Total Carbohydrate	7 g
Dietary Fiber	2 g
Sugars	1 g
Protein	2 g

Combine all ingredients in a blender or food processor. Process until smooth.

Preparation time: 8 minutes

Time flies. It's up to you to be the navigator.
—Robert Orben

Sun-Dried Tomato and Basil Dip

12 servings/serving size: 2 Tbsp

This creamy dip can also be used as a salad dressing. Just thin out the mixture with some nonfat milk or low-fat buttermilk and mix until smooth and creamy.

1 cup low-fat ricotta cheese
4 sun-dried tomatoes, rehydrated and finely minced (Avoid using the sun-dried tomatoes in oil. It is very difficult to remove the high-fat oil from the tomatoes.)
2 garlic cloves, finely minced
1 tsp finely minced chives
1 Tbsp finely minced basil
1 tsp olive oil

Vegetable Exchange	1
Calories	33
Total Fat	1 g
Saturated Fat	1 g
Calories from Fat	10
Cholesterol	8 mg
Sodium	104 mg
Total Carbohydrate	3 g
Dietary Fiber	0 g
Sugars	1 g
Protein	4 g

Combine all ingredients by hand in a small bowl. Refrigerate until serving time, or about 2 hours. This dip is very good served with crackers or raw vegetables.

Preparation time: 8 minutes

Spinach Dip

12 servings/serving size: 2 Tbsp

If you let the spinach defrost in the refrigerator, you can avoid spending time cooking it. You can also use this dip to top broiled salmon steaks.

1 10-oz package frozen chopped spinach or broccoli, thawed
2 Tbsp red wine vinegar
3 garlic cloves, minced
1 Tbsp fresh minced mint
1 cup low-fat sour cream
Fresh ground pepper to taste

Vegetable Exchange	1
Calories	26
Total Fat	2 g
Saturated Fat	1 g
Calories from Fat	14
Cholesterol	7 mg
Sodium	24 mg
Total Carbohydrate	2 g
Dietary Fiber	1 g
Sugars	1 g
Protein	1 g

Drain the defrosted spinach and press out all the water until the spinach is very dry. Combine all ingredients by hand. Refrigerate for 2 hours. Serve inside a hollowed-out, round loaf of bread, and surround with crackers, breadsticks, vegetables, or pita wedges.

Preparation time: 7 minutes

White Bean Pate

12 servings/serving size: 2 Tbsp

This spread resembles the wonderfully aromatic French boursin cheese, but contains much less fat.

1/2 cup minced scallions
3 garlic cloves, minced
1 15-oz can white beans (navy or cannelini)
2 tsp prepared Dijon mustard
1 Tbsp fresh lemon juice
1 tsp olive oil
2 Tbsp minced parsley
1 Tbsp minced basil
1 tsp minced thyme leaves
1 tsp minced dill
1 tsp minced tarragon
1/4 tsp nutmeg
Fresh ground pepper and salt to taste

Starch Exchange	1/2
Calories	49
Total Fat	1 g
Saturated Fat	0 g
Calories from Fat	5
Cholesterol	0 mg
Sodium	165 mg
Total Carbohydrate	9 g
Dietary Fiber	2 g
Sugars	1 g
Protein	3 g

Combine all ingredients in a blender or food processor. Process until smooth. Serve with crackers or pita bread.

Preparation time: 10 minutes

Sesame Basil Chicken Tidbits

6 servings/serving size: 2 oz

These tender little chicken bites can be made ahead of time and reheated at the last moment. Since the chicken has been marinated, it will not lose its moistness.

Chicken:
3/4 lb boneless, skinless chicken
   breasts

Marinade:
3 Tbsp lite soy sauce
2 tsp sesame oil
2 Tbsp dry sherry
2 Tbsp fresh orange juice
2 Tbsp minced fresh basil
1 Tbsp toasted sesame seeds
2 dried red chilies
Red leaf lettuce to line platter

Very Lean Meat	
Exchange	2
Calories	79
Total Fat	2 g
Saturated Fat	1 g
Calories from Fat	20
Cholesterol	34 mg
Sodium	131 mg
Total Carbohydrate	1 g
Dietary Fiber	0 g
Sugars	1 g
Protein	13 g

1. Cut the chicken breasts into 2-inch cubes.
2. Combine all the marinade ingredients and mix well. Add the cubed chicken and marinate at least 2 hours.
3. Remove the chicken cubes from the marinade and place on a broiler rack. Broil 2–3 minutes per side until chicken is cooked throughout.
4. Serve on a lettuce-lined platter with fancy frill toothpicks.

Preparation time: 13 minutes

Fresh Tomato Bruschetta

6 servings/serving size: 1 oz

This is the simplest of appetizers, yet elegant enough for any party.

Bread:
1 6-oz loaf Italian or French bread
1 Tbsp olive oil

Topping:
2 plum tomatoes, minced (or 1 salad tomato)
3 garlic cloves, minced
2 tsp minced basil
1 tsp minced thyme
2 tsp olive oil

Starch Exchange	1
Monounsaturated Fat Exchange	1
Calories	118
Total Fat	4 g
Saturated Fat	0 g
Calories from Fat	22
Cholesterol	0 mg
Sodium	156 mg
Total Carbohydrate	16 g
Dietary Fiber	2 g
Sugars	2 g
Protein	2 g

1. Preheat the oven to 350 degrees. Cut the bread into 6 even slices. Brush each slice with olive oil and place onto a cookie sheet.
2. To prepare the topping, combine all ingredients.
3. Place the bread in the oven and toast for 1–2 minutes.
4. Remove the bread from the oven and spread a teaspoon of topping over each slice. Serve immediately.

Preparation time: 10 minutes

Spiced Scallops

6 servings/serving size: about 2 oz

Zippy spices jazz up mild bay scallops.

Scallops:
3/4 lb bay scallops

Spice mixture:
2 Tbsp fresh lemon juice
1 medium onion, chopped
3 garlic cloves, minced
1/4 cup minced parsley
3 tsp cumin
1 tsp cayenne pepper
1 tsp coriander
Fresh ground pepper to taste
Tabasco sauce to taste

Very Lean Meat	
Exchange	1
Calories	50
Total Fat	0 g
Saturated Fat	0 g
Calories from Fat	4
Cholesterol	18 mg
Sodium	92 mg
Total Carbohydrate	2 g
Dietary Fiber	0 g
Sugars	1 g
Protein	9 g

1. Combine all ingredients for spice mixture. Toss the scallops in the mixture. Let them marinate for 20 minutes.
2. In a steamer over boiling water, steam the scallops about 2 minutes. Remove from heat.
3. Place the scallops on a plate and spear with toothpicks. Serve immediately.

Preparation time: 10 minutes

Oriental Ginger Pork

6 servings/serving size: 2 oz with 1 Tbsp sauce

Keep a good supply of napkins ready for this fun-to-eat appetizer!

Pork:
1 lb lean pork tenderloin, trimmed and ground (your butcher will do this for you)
2 garlic cloves, minced
1 tsp ground ginger
1 tsp lite soy sauce

Sauce:
1/4 cup rice vinegar
1/2 cup lite soy sauce
1/4 cup tomato paste
2 Tbsp honey
1 Tbsp Tabasco sauce

Very Lean Meat Exchange	2
Starch Exchange	1/2
Calories	107
Total Fat	3 g
Saturated Fat	1 g
Calories from Fat	25
Cholesterol	44 mg
Sodium	341 mg
Total Carbohydrate	4 g
Dietary Fiber	0 g
Sugars	3 g
Protein	16 g

1. Preheat the oven to 350 degrees. Combine the pork with the garlic, ginger, and soy sauce. Form into 2-inch meatballs.
2. Combine all sauce ingredients and set aside.
3. Place meatballs in a baking dish and bake for 20 minutes. Add the sauce and bake for 10 more minutes. Serve meatballs speared with toothpicks.

Preparation time: 15 minutes

Soup's On!

Serving a hearty soup is a great way to get a meal on the table in no time flat. Just add cooked or raw vegetables and some crusty bread to complete the meal! All of the following soups can be frozen for future use. You can freeze soup in heavy-duty ziploc freezer bags or 1-quart containers. To reheat the soup, defrost it in the microwave first on the defrost setting and then continue to heat until the soup is at the desired temperature.

All of these soups make use of canned low-fat, low-sodium broths. When you have more time, consider making your own broth. When you shop for canned broth, look for a brand that is clear broth with very little fat resting on the top when you open it. Any leftover broth can be saved for future use. Just pour it into ice cube trays and freeze. When recipes call for broth, just pop out a cube (about 1 Tbsp each).

Grab a bowl and savor these fresh homemade soups!

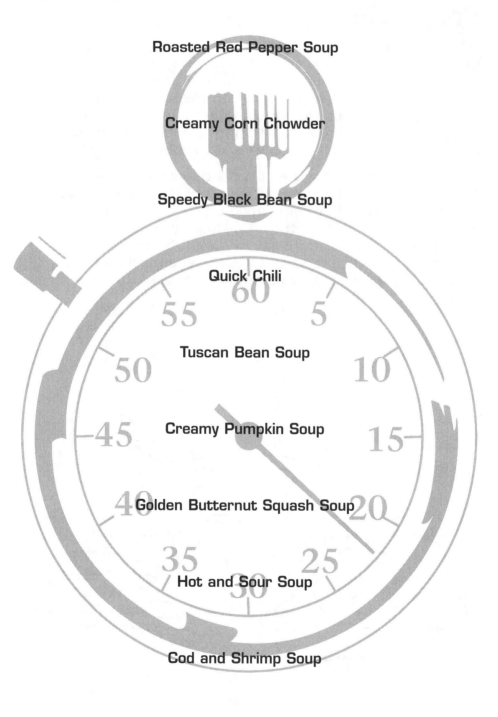

Roasted Red Pepper Soup

Creamy Corn Chowder

Speedy Black Bean Soup

Quick Chili

Tuscan Bean Soup

Creamy Pumpkin Soup

Golden Butternut Squash Soup

Hot and Sour Soup

Cod and Shrimp Soup

30

Roasted Red Pepper Soup

6 servings/serving size: 1 cup

Serve this rosy red soup any time of the year.

Soup:
1 medium onion, chopped
4 garlic cloves, minced
2 Tbsp olive oil
3 roasted red peppers or 1 7-oz jar
   (roasted red peppers in a jar are in
   the grocery store condiment aisle)
3 cups low-fat, low-sodium chicken
   broth
1/2 cup tomato juice
Fresh ground pepper to taste

Garnish:
Paper-thin lemon slices
Parsley sprigs
Fresh ground pepper to taste

Starch Exchange	1/2
Monounsaturated Fat Exchange	1
Calories	80
Total Fat	6 g
Saturated Fat	1 g
Calories from Fat	54
Cholesterol	0 mg
Sodium	300 mg
Total Carbohydrate	7 g
Dietary Fiber	1 g
Sugars	6 g
Protein	3 g

1. In a small skillet over medium-high heat, heat the oil. Add the onion and garlic and saute for 5 minutes. Do not let garlic turn brown. Remove from heat.
2. In a blender or food processor, place the garlic onion mixture and the roasted red peppers. Puree until smooth.
3. In a stockpot over high heat, bring the broth to a boil. Lower the heat to medium and add the roasted pepper puree. Stir until smooth. Add the tomato juice and simmer for 10 minutes. Add the pepper.
4. To serve, pour soup into soup bowls. Place 2 slices of lemon per bowl in the center of the bowl. Top with a parsley sprig. Grind more black pepper on top. Serve immediately.

Creamy Corn Chowder

6 servings/serving size: 1 cup

This chowder is rich and satisfying. In the summer, use fresh corn scraped right off the cob.

Chowder:
1 tsp olive oil
1 medium onion, chopped
1 medium potato, peeled and cubed
1 cup low-fat, low-sodium chicken
  broth
2 cups corn kernels
2 cups evaporated skimmed milk
2 Tbsp cornstarch or arrowroot
4 Tbsp cold water
Fresh ground pepper to taste
1 tsp liquid smoke (optional)

Garnish:
2 Tbsp minced parsley

Starch Exchange	2
Calories	156
Total Fat	1 g
Saturated Fat	0 g
Calories from Fat	13
Cholesterol	3 mg
Sodium	121 mg
Total Carbohydrate	29 g
Dietary Fiber	2 g
Sugars	10 g
Protein	9 g

1. In a nonstick stockpot, heat the oil. Add the onion and saute for 5 minutes. Add the diced potato and 1/2 cup of the broth. Cook for 10 minutes until potato is soft.
2. Add the corn, milk, and remaining broth and simmer over medium heat for 15 minutes.
3. Combine the cornstarch and water. Add to the soup and cook over low heat until soup is thickened. Add liquid smoke, if desired. Garnish with parsley.

Speedy Black Bean Soup

6 servings/serving size: 1 cup

There are many versions of Black Bean Soup available, but this one is probably the fastest around. No vegetables are included, except onion, so if you want to include more vegetables, the soup will take a little longer to cook.

Soup:
1 tsp olive oil
1 small onion, minced
2 15-oz cans black beans, 1 can drained
1 1/2 cups low-fat, low-sodium chicken broth
1/2 cup dry red wine
Fresh ground pepper to taste
1 tsp cayenne pepper

Garnish:
6 Tbsp low-fat sour cream
Cilantro or parsley sprigs

Very Lean Meat Exchange	1
Starch Exchange	1 1/2
Calories	168
Total Fat	3 g
Saturated Fat	1 g
Calories from Fat	27
Cholesterol	5 mg
Sodium	394 mg
Total Carbohydrate	26 g
Dietary Fiber	8 g
Sugars	4 g
Protein	10 g

1. In a stockpot over medium-high heat, heat the oil. Add the onion and saute for 5 minutes.
2. Add the drained can of beans and chicken broth. Simmer for 5 minutes.
3. Puree the other can of beans with the bean liquid in a blender or food processor. Add to the soup. Add the red wine, ground pepper, and cayenne pepper and simmer for 10 minutes. Garnish with sour cream and parsley or cilantro sprigs.

Preparation time: 15 minutes

Quick Chili

6 servings/serving size: 1 cup

True chili is actually prepared without beans. This soup simmers just long enough for the flavors to blend.

2 tsp olive oil
1 medium onion, chopped
1 small red pepper, chopped
4 cloves garlic, minced
1 lb lean pork tenderloin, trimmed and ground (your butcher will do this for you)
3 Tbsp ground chili powder
1 tsp cinnamon
1/2 tsp allspice
2 cups canned tomatoes, coarsely chopped, undrained
2 cups low-sodium beef broth
1 Tbsp red wine
1 Tbsp Worcestershire sauce
Fresh ground pepper to taste

Lean Meat Exchange	2
Starch Exchange	1/2
Calories	160
Total Fat	6 g
Saturated Fat	1 g
Calories from Fat	53
Cholesterol	44 mg
Sodium	262 mg
Total Carbohydrate	11 g
Dietary Fiber	3 g
Sugars	5 g
Protein	18 g

Preparation time: 20 minutes

1. In a stockpot over medium-high heat, heat the oil. Add the onion and pepper and saute for 5 minutes. Add the garlic and saute for 2 minutes. Add the pork and saute for 5 minutes.
2. Add the remaining ingredients and simmer over medium-low heat for 20 minutes.

Tuscan Bean Soup

6 servings/serving size: 1 cup

This hearty soup, plus bread and salad, is all you need for a filling meal.

1 Tbsp olive oil
1 medium onion, minced
2 garlic cloves, minced
1 medium red pepper, chopped
3 cups low-fat, low-sodium chicken broth
1 cup coarsely chopped canned tomatoes
1 1/2 cups canned red kidney beans, cannelini beans, or navy beans, drained
2 tsp chopped fresh thyme
1/2 cup chopped spinach or escarole
1 cup cooked small pasta shells
Fresh ground pepper to taste

Starch Exchange	2
Monounsaturated Fat Exchange	1/2
Calories	184
Total Fat	6 g
Saturated Fat	1 g
Calories from Fat	56
Cholesterol	0 mg
Sodium	212 mg
Total Carbohydrate	27 g
Dietary Fiber	4 g
Sugars	5 g
Protein	8 g

1. In a stockpot over medium-high heat, heat the oil. Add the onion and garlic and saute for 5 minutes. Add the pepper and saute for 3 more minutes.
2. Add the broth, tomatoes, and beans. Bring to a boil. Simmer over low heat for 20 minutes.
3. Add the thyme, spinach, and cooked pasta. Simmer for 5 more minutes. Grind in pepper to taste and serve.

Preparation time: 15 minutes

Creamy Pumpkin Soup

6 servings/serving size: 1 cup

Pumpkin seeds are lower in fat than some other kinds of seeds. Just a few add taste and texture to this marvelous, creamy soup.

1/4 cup pumpkin seeds
2 tsp canola oil
1 medium onion, chopped
1 1/2 cups canned pumpkin
3 1/2 cups low-fat, low-sodium chicken broth
1 cup evaporated skim milk
2 Tbsp dry sherry
1 tsp cinnamon
Fresh ground pepper to taste

Starch Exchange	1
Fat Exchange	1 1/2
Calories	142
Total Fat	7 g
Saturated Fat	1 g
Calories from Fat	64
Cholesterol	2 mg
Sodium	115 mg
Total Carbohydrate	14 g
Dietary Fiber	3 g
Sugars	8 g
Protein	9 g

1. Preheat the oven to 400 degrees. Spread the pumpkin seeds on a small cookie sheet. Drizzle 1 tsp of the canola oil on the seeds and toast the seeds for 5 minutes. Remove from the oven.
2. In a stockpot, heat the remaining oil. Add the onion and saute for 5 minutes. Add the pumpkin and broth and bring to a boil. Simmer for 20 minutes. Add the milk, sherry, and cinnamon. Simmer for 5 minutes.
3. To serve, place soup in bowls and top with pumpkin seeds. Grind pepper over each serving.

Preparation time: 15 minutes

Golden Butternut Squash Soup

6 servings/serving size: 1 cup

Butternut squash is a great source of Vitamin A. If you use frozen butternut squash, you will save considerable cooking time. If you prefer fresh squash or when you have more time, use 1 1/2 lb cubed raw butternut squash and cook the soup for 45 minutes.

1 tsp canola oil
1 small onion, minced
1 carrot, peeled and diced
2 10-oz packages butternut squash, thawed
1 cup low-fat, low-sodium chicken broth
1 1/2 cups evaporated skim milk
1 tsp nutmeg
Fresh ground pepper to taste

Starch Exchange	1
Vegetable Exchange	1
Calories	110
Total Fat	1 g
Saturated Fat	0 g
Calories from Fat	13
Cholesterol	2 mg
Sodium	107 mg
Total Carbohydrate	20 g
Dietary Fiber	3 g
Sugars	9 g
Protein	7 g

1. In a stockpot over medium-high heat, heat the oil. Add the onion and saute for 3 minutes. Add the carrot and saute for 3 more minutes. Add the butternut squash and broth and bring to a boil.
2. Add the milk and simmer on low heat for 20 minutes.
3. Add the nutmeg. In batches, puree the soup in a blender until smooth. Add pepper to taste. Serve immediately.

Preparation time: 15 minutes

Hot and Sour Soup

6 servings/serving size: 1 cup

The traditional great taste, but less fat and fewer calories!

4 cups low-fat, low-sodium chicken
  broth
4 Tbsp white vinegar
2 Tbsp lite soy sauce
1 Tbsp crushed red pepper
2 tsp sesame oil
1 cup sliced mushrooms
1 cup thinly sliced carrot
2 tsp cornstarch or arrowroot
4 tsp water

Starch Exchange	1/2
Fat Exchange	1/2
Calories	50
Total Fat	3 g
Saturated Fat	1 g
Calories from Fat	28
Cholesterol	0 mg
Sodium	288 mg
Total Carbohydrate	6 g
Dietary Fiber	1 g
Sugars	3 g
Protein	3 g

1. In a stockpot, combine the broth, vinegar, soy sauce, crushed red pepper, and sesame oil. Bring to a boil, then simmer for 10 minutes.
2. Add the mushrooms and carrots and simmer for 10 more minutes.
3. Combine the cornstarch or arrowroot with the water. Add to the soup and continue to cook for 5 minutes, until it thickens.

Preparation time: 12 minutes

Time wounds all heels.
—Groucho Marx

Cod and Shrimp Soup

6 servings/serving size: 1 cup with 3 oz seafood

Use this soup as a first course before pasta, or with fresh bread and salad for a nutritious meal.

2 tsp olive oil
1 medium onion, minced
3 garlic cloves, minced
1 small red pepper, diced
2 cups canned tomatoes, coarsely
    chopped, undrained
1 cup sliced okra
1 1/2 cups low-fat, low-sodium chicken
    broth
1 tsp chili powder
1 tsp celery seed
2 tsp paprika
2 Tbsp tomato paste
3/4 lb cod fillets, cubed
2/3 lb shelled and deveined medium
    shrimp

Very Lean Meat	
Exchange	3
Starch Exchange	1
Calories	166
Total Fat	4 g
Saturated Fat	1 g
Calories from Fat	34
Cholesterol	98 mg
Sodium	268 mg
Total Carbohydrate	12 g
Dietary Fiber	3 g
Sugars	6 g
Protein	23 g

1. In a stockpot, heat the oil. Add the onion and garlic and saute for 3 minutes. Add the red pepper and saute 3 more minutes.
2. Add all the remaining ingredients except the seafood. Simmer over low heat for 20 minutes.
3. Add the cod and shrimp and cover. Cook for 5 more minutes. Serve immediately.

Preparation time: 15 minutes

Super Salads

Today a salad means more than just a wedge of iceberg lettuce and Thousand Island salad dressing! By being creative with different kinds of vegetables, you can turn a hum-drum salad into a culinary feast.

Including a fresh salad every day in your meal plan increases your fiber intake. Always try to include dark greens first, such as spinach and romaine lettuce, when choosing salad ingredients.

The culprit that turns relatively healthy salads into diet disasters is too much fat from the dressings. Enliven the flavor of your salads with interesting vinegars and fresh herbs instead. The traditional ratio of oil to vinegar is two to one. Reverse that proportion to make an equally delicious, but much lower-fat, salad dressing. Feel free to experiment: try using only vinegar and lots of herbs. You may be surprised to find you don't miss the oil at all!

Dressings should not overpower a salad. Instead, just use a fine mist or splash of dressing to wake up greens. If you find you need more dressing to coat your salad, increase the proportion of nonfat ingredients only, such as the juices and vinegars.

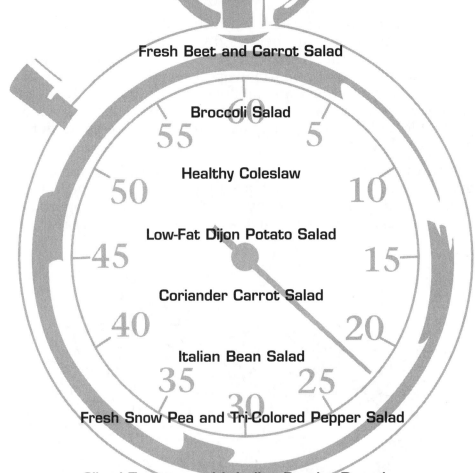

Arugula and Watercress Salad

Walnut-Flavored Artichoke and Grapefruit Salad

Spinach Orange Salad

Fresh Beet and Carrot Salad

Broccoli Salad

Healthy Coleslaw

Low-Fat Dijon Potato Salad

Coriander Carrot Salad

Italian Bean Salad

Fresh Snow Pea and Tri-Colored Pepper Salad

Sliced Tomatoes with Italian Parsley Dressing

Arugula and Watercress Salad

6 servings/serving size: 1 cup

A great-tasting salad with a bite!

Dressing:
2 Tbsp olive oil
3 Tbsp sherry vinegar
1 Tbsp Dijon mustard
1 Tbsp orange juice
2 tsp grated orange peel
Fresh ground pepper and salt to taste

Salad:
4 cups arugula, washed and torn
2 cups watercress, washed and torn
1 red onion, sliced into thin rings
1/2 cup halved cherry tomatoes

Garnish:
2 Tbsp toasted sesame seeds

Monounsaturated Fat Exchange	1
Vegetable Exchange	1
Calories	80
Total Fat	6 g
Saturated Fat	1 g
Calories from Fat	56
Cholesterol	0 mg
Sodium	66 mg
Total Carbohydrate	5 g
Dietary Fiber	1 g
Sugars	3 g
Protein	2 g

1. Combine all dressing ingredients in a small bowl. Whisk until blended.
2. In a salad bowl, toss all ingredients for the salad. Add dressing and toss well.
3. Top each individual salad plate with toasted sesame seeds.

Preparation time: 8 minutes

Walnut-Flavored Artichoke and Grapefruit Salad

6 servings/serving size: 1 cup

The delicate, yet robust, flavor of walnut oil gives this salad a gourmet touch.

1 15-oz can artichoke hearts, drained
2 Tbsp walnut oil
3 Tbsp white wine vinegar
1 Tbsp minced parsley
1 Tbsp minced scallions
4 cups combined romaine lettuce leaves and endive leaves, washed and torn
1 large pink grapefruit, separated into sections

Polyunsaturated Fat Exchange	1
Vegetable Exchange	1
Fruit Exchange	1/2
Calories	82
Total Fat	5 g
Saturated Fat	0 g
Calories from Fat	44
Cholesterol	0 mg
Sodium	122 mg
Total Carbohydrate	9 g
Dietary Fiber	3 g
Sugars	5 g
Protein	2 g

1. Combine the walnut oil, vinegar, parsley, and scallions in a blender. Process 15 seconds. Toss artichoke hearts into the dressing and refrigerate while you prepare the lettuce and grapefruit.
2. Place the lettuce leaves and endive on individual plates or in a large salad bowl. Place the grapefruit sections in a star pattern over the lettuce. Pile the marinated artichokes on top.

Preparation time: 10 minutes

Spinach Orange Salad

6 servings/serving size: 1 cup

Try to include a dark salad green like spinach in your meal plan every day.

Dressing:
2 Tbsp canola oil
3 Tbsp orange juice
1 Tbsp lemon juice
1 tsp grated orange peel
Fresh ground pepper and salt to taste

Salad:
5 cups torn fresh spinach leaves,
   washed and dried
1/2 cup mandarin oranges, packed in
    their own juice, drained
1/2 cup thinly sliced dried apricots
1 small red onion, thinly sliced
1 Tbsp toasted pine nuts

Monounsaturated Fat Exchange	1
Vegetable Exchange	1
Fruit Exchange	1/2
Calories	**105**
Total Fat	**6 g**
Saturated Fat	1 g
Calories from Fat	52
Cholesterol	**0 mg**
Sodium	**63 mg**
Total Carbohydrate	**13 g**
Dietary Fiber	3 g
Sugars	8 g
Protein	**3 g**

Whisk all dressing ingredients together and set aside. In a large salad bowl, toss together the salad ingredients. Add the dressing and toss to coat. Serve immediately.

Preparation time: 10 minutes

Fresh Beet and Carrot Salad

6 servings/serving size: 1 cup

Grated fresh beets are delicious to eat, and their red color adds eye appeal to this crunchy salad.

Salad:
3 cups grated fresh beets (about 3–4 medium beets), peeled and uncooked
2 cups grated raw carrots, peeled
1 cup grated raw zucchini, unpeeled

Dressing:
1/2 cup rice vinegar
2 Tbsp sesame oil
1 Tbsp grated ginger
1 Tbsp dry sherry
Fresh ground pepper and salt to taste
Romaine lettuce leaves to line salad bowl or individual plates

Vegetable Exchange	2
Fat Exchange	1
Calories	95
Total Fat	5 g
Saturated Fat	1 g
Calories from Fat	42
Cholesterol	0 mg
Sodium	90 mg
Total Carbohydrate	12 g
Dietary Fiber	3 g
Sugars	8 g
Protein	2 g

1. In a large bowl, toss together the grated beets, carrots, and zucchini.
2. In a blender, combine the dressing ingredients. Add to the beets and toss well.
3. Place the romaine lettuce leaves on individual plates or in a large salad bowl. Pile on the beet mixture and serve.

Preparation time: 15 minutes

Broccoli Salad

6 servings/serving size: 1 cup

This broccoli salad goes very well with any Asian food.

Salad:
6 cups broccoli florets (about 2–3 lb)
2 quarts water

Dressing:
1 Tbsp corn oil
2 Tbsp sesame oil
3 Tbsp lite soy sauce
1/2 cup minced scallions
3 garlic cloves, minced

Polyunsaturated Fat
  Exchange 1 1/2
Vegetable Exchange 1
Calories 95
Total Fat .... 7 g
  Saturated Fat .... 1 g
  Calories from Fat 66
Cholesterol .... 0 mg
Sodium .... 328 mg
Total Carbohydrate .... 6 g
  Dietary Fiber .... 3 g
  Sugars .... 3 g
Protein .... 3 g

1. In a large pot, bring the water to a boil. Add the broccoli and blanch for 2–3 minutes. Immediately drain the broccoli and then plunge it in a bowl of ice water to stop the cooking process. Drain again. Place in a large salad bowl.
2. Combine the dressing ingredients. Add the blanched broccoli and toss well. Refrigerate until ready to serve.

Preparation time: 10 minutes

Healthy Coleslaw

6 servings/serving size: 1 cup

Cabbage is a great basic vegetable to add to soups, salads, or stir-fry because of its unique, tangy flavor. When stored properly, cabbage can last up to two weeks.

Salad:
3 cups shredded green cabbage (1/2 medium head)
2 cups shredded red cabbage
1 cup shredded carrot
1/2 cup golden raisins

Dressing:
1/3 cup low-fat mayonnaise
1/4 cup plain low-fat yogurt
2 Tbsp apple juice concentrate
2 Tbsp poppy seeds
2 Tbsp red wine vinegar

Polyunsaturated Fat Exchange	1
Vegetable Exchange	1
Fruit Exchange	1
Calories	135
Total Fat	6 g
Saturated Fat	1 g
Calories from Fat	52
Cholesterol	6 mg
Sodium	123 mg
Total Carbohydrate	19 g
Dietary Fiber	3 g
Sugars	15 g
Protein	3 g

1. Combine the cabbage, carrot, and raisins in a large bowl. Toss well.
2. Combine all the dressing ingredients. Add the dressing to the cabbage mixture and toss well. Refrigerate until ready to serve.

Preparation time: 15 minutes

Low-Fat Dijon Potato Salad

6 servings/serving size: 1/2 cup

Low-fat buttermilk and Dijon mustard give this salad a great flavor, with much less fat!

Salad:
1 lb red potatoes, unpeeled and cubed
1/2 cup diagonally sliced celery
1/4 cup sliced scallions
2 Tbsp chopped shallots

Dressing:
1/2 cup low-fat buttermilk
2 Tbsp low-fat mayonnaise
1 Tbsp Dijon mustard
1 Tbsp tarragon vinegar

Starch Exchange	1
Polyunsaturated Fat	
Exchange	1/2
Calories	97
Total Fat	2 g
Saturated Fat	0 g
Calories from Fat	17
Cholesterol	3 mg
Sodium	103 mg
Total Carbohydrate	18 g
Dietary Fiber	2 g
Sugars	3 g
Protein	2 g

1. In a medium-size pot, cover the cubed potatoes with water. Bring to a boil, lower the heat, and cook on medium heat until potatoes are tender, yet firm (about 15 minutes).
2. Toss cooked potatoes with celery, scallions, and shallots.
3. In a small bowl, combine all dressing ingredients. Add to the potato salad and mix well. Refrigerate until ready to serve.

Coriander Carrot Salad

6 servings/serving size: 1 cup

This salad will keep in the refrigerator for several days. It's a little spicy!

Salad:
3 large carrots, peeled and grated
3 Tbsp chopped shallots
2 Tbsp minced parsley

Dressing:
2 Tbsp olive oil
3 Tbsp fresh lemon juice
2 tsp cumin
1 Tbsp coriander seeds
1 tsp turmeric
Dash cayenne pepper
Fresh ground pepper to taste

Monounsaturated Fat Exchange	1
Vegetable Exchange	2
Calories	81
Total Fat	5 g
Saturated Fat	1 g
Calories from Fat	42
Cholesterol	0 mg
Sodium	32 mg
Total Carbohydrate	10 g
Dietary Fiber	3 g
Sugars	6 g
Protein	1 g

Combine the grated carrots, shallots, and parsley in a large salad bowl. Whisk together the dressing ingredients. Toss the dressing with the carrots. Refrigerate until ready to serve.

Preparation time: 15 minutes

Italian Bean Salad

6 servings/serving size: 1/2 cup

Earthy balsamic vinegar dribbled over this hearty salad gives it a special flavor.

2 15-oz cans white beans, drained
1 small red onion, minced
3 stalks celery, diagonally sliced
1/4 cup sliced scallions
1/2 cup minced parsley
2 Tbsp balsamic vinegar
1 Tbsp olive oil
Fresh ground pepper to taste

Starch Exchange	2
Calories	167
Total Fat	3 g
Saturated Fat	0 g
Calories from Fat	26
Cholesterol	0 mg
Sodium	188 mg
Total Carbohydrate	28 g
Dietary Fiber	5 g
Sugars	4 g
Protein	9 g

Combine all ingredients in the order given. Add more balsamic vinegar if desired. Refrigerate until ready to serve.

Preparation time: 10 minutes

I must govern the clock, not be governed by it.
—Golda Meir

Fresh Snow Pea and Tri-Colored Pepper Salad

6 servings/serving size: about 1 cup

This salad is almost too pretty to eat.

Salad:
2 quarts water
1 each small green, red, and yellow peppers, cored and sliced thin
1/4 lb fresh snow peas, trimmed
1/2 cup halved cherry tomatoes

Dressing:
3 Tbsp balsamic vinegar
1 Tbsp minced shallot
1 Tbsp olive oil
2 tsp fresh lemon juice
2 tsp Dijon mustard
Fresh ground pepper and salt to taste

Monounsaturated Fat Exchange	1/2
Vegetable Exchange	1
Calories	55
Total Fat	3 g
Saturated Fat	0 g
Calories from Fat	23
Cholesterol	0 mg
Sodium	49 mg
Total Carbohydrate	8 g
Dietary Fiber	2 g
Sugars	5 g
Protein	2 g

1. In a large pot, bring the water to a boil. Add the sliced peppers and blanch for 2 minutes. Add the snow peas and blanch 30 seconds more. Drain. Plunge the peppers and snow peas into ice water to stop the cooking process. Drain again.
2. In a large salad bowl, toss the blanched peppers and snow peas with the cherry tomatoes.
3. Combine the dressing ingredients in a small bowl. Add the dressing to the pepper mixture and toss well. Refrigerate until ready to serve.

Preparation time: 12 minutes

Sliced Tomatoes with Italian Parsley Dressing

6 servings/serving size: 1 cup

This salad can be assembled right before serving.

Salad:
2–3 large, ripe salad tomatoes

Dressing:
1/2 cup minced parsley
2 Tbsp minced fresh basil
3 Tbsp olive oil
2 Tbsp lemon juice
4 garlic cloves, minced
Fresh ground pepper and salt to taste

Monounsaturated Fat Exchange	1 1/2
Vegetable Exchange	1
Calories	90
Total Fat	7 g
Saturated Fat	1 g
Calories from Fat	65
Cholesterol	0 mg
Sodium	38 mg
Total Carbohydrate	7 g
Dietary Fiber	2 g
Sugars	4 g
Protein	1 g

1. Slice the tomatoes and place them on a platter in an overlapping pattern.
2. In a blender or food processor, combine the dressing ingredients. Drizzle the dressing over the tomatoes just prior to serving.

Preparation time: 10 minutes

Vegetarian Fare

Vegetarian cooking is more sophisticated and interesting today than back in the hippie days of the 1960s! Eating vegetarian food has many benefits. The high-fiber content of most dishes makes them ideal to aid in weight control and good for the digestive system, too. Grains and pastas are still relatively inexpensive and are well-liked by almost everyone.

Try to purchase good pasta, like imported Italian varieties made from hard durum semolina wheat—it cooks up nice and firm, and is tastier than American wheat. Look for whole-wheat varieties for a nuttier taste. Try brown rice instead of white for a bit more fiber and a much better flavor.

In these recipes assume that the 1-cup serving size is for a main dish. To serve as a side dish, reduce the serving size to 1/2 cup.

Pick up a fork and dig into these nutritious, hearty, and delicious dishes!

Tips for Success

Sesame Noodles

Pasta Puttanesca

Rigatoni with Eggplant and Mushrooms

Shells Agli Olio

Angel Hair Pasta with Tomato Seafood Cream Sauce

Moroccan Couscous with Chickpeas

Couscous Tabouli

Vegetable Rice and Beans

Indian Rice Curry

Two-Tone Rice Pilaf

55 60 5
50 10
45 15
40 20
35 25
30

56

Tips for Success

Since brown rice does take longer to cook than white rice, follow these steps for preparing it and freezing it so you will
always have it on hand.

Prepare the rice by first rinsing it under water in a colander.
Boil double the amount of liquid (water or broth) in a
saucepan. Add your rinsed rice slowly to the pan, bring to a
boil, cover, lower the heat, and cook for 45 minutes until the
water is absorbed. Do not stir while cooking—this loosens the
starch and causes the grain to become very gummy.

Place the cooked rice in heavy-duty ziploc bags (the 1-quart
size is best) and freeze. When you're ready to use it, place the
bag in the microwave. On the defrost setting, defrost rice for
about 8 minutes, just until it breaks up. Then reheat the rice
gently either in the microwave or on the stovetop until it's hot.

There are also couscous recipes included in this chapter.
Couscous is very easy to work with. Simply rehydrate couscous
in double the amount of liquid. It will rehydrate in as little as
five minutes and is ready to go. Almost all supermarkets now
carry couscous.

You can use canned beans in this chapter's recipes. Just thoroughly rinse the beans to remove excess sodium. Beans are a
great source of dietary fiber, too.

Sesame Noodles

6 servings/serving size: 1 cup

A favorite with the Chinese take-out crowd, this dish is easy to make at home.

1 Tbsp peanut butter
2 Tbsp lite soy sauce
1 tsp sesame oil
3 garlic cloves, minced
1 tsp grated ginger
2 cups cooked thin spaghetti noodles
1/2 cup thinly sliced red pepper
1/2 cup thinly sliced carrots
1/4 cup minced scallions
1/4 cup bean sprouts
Red pepper flakes

Starch Exchange	1
Fat Exchange	1/2
Calories	102
Total Fat	2 g
Saturated Fat	0 g
Calories from Fat	22
Cholesterol	0 mg
Sodium	219 mg
Total Carbohydrate	17 g
Dietary Fiber	2 g
Sugars	3 g
Protein	3 g

1. In a small saucepan, combine the peanut butter, soy sauce, sesame oil, garlic, and ginger. Bring the mixture to a boil, reduce the heat, and simmer for 3 minutes.
2. Combine the remaining ingredients and pour the hot peanut sesame dressing over the pasta vegetable mixture. Serve immediately, or chill and serve cold.

Preparation time: 17 minutes

Pasta Puttanesca

6 servings/serving size: 1 cup pasta with about 1/2 cup vegetables and sauce

This very traditional olive tomato sauce gets a bit lighter by using more vegetables and just a few olives.

Sauce:
2 tsp olive oil
1 medium onion, chopped
4 garlic cloves, minced
2 carrots, peeled and diced
1 28-oz can plum tomatoes, coarsely chopped, undrained
2 Tbsp white wine
2 Tbsp minced basil
2 Tbsp chopped black olives
2 tsp capers
6 cups cooked fusilli (corkscrew) pasta

Garnish:
2 Tbsp minced parsley
2 Tbsp grated Parmesan cheese

Starch Exchange	3
Vegetable Exchange	1
Calories	276
Total Fat	4 g
Saturated Fat	1 g
Calories from Fat	32
Cholesterol	1 mg
Sodium	283 mg
Total Carbohydrate	52 g
Dietary Fiber	5 g
Sugars	8 g
Protein	9 g

1. In a heavy skillet over medium heat, heat the oil. Saute the onion and garlic for 5 minutes. Add the carrots and continue to saute for 5 more minutes.
2. Add the tomatoes and white wine and bring to a boil. Lower the heat and simmer for 15 minutes.
3. Add the basil, olives, and capers and simmer for 5 more minutes.
4. Toss the cooked fusilli with the sauce. Garnish with parsley and grated Parmesan cheese as desired.

Rigatoni with Eggplant and Mushrooms

6 servings/serving size: 1 cup pasta with about 2/3 cup vegetables and sauce

This very filling vegetarian dish needs only a salad and warm bread to complete it.

Sauce:
1 Tbsp olive oil
1/4 cup dry white wine
3 garlic cloves, minced
1 red onion, chopped
1 cup diced eggplant, unpeeled
1 cup sliced mushrooms
1 28-oz can plum tomatoes, coarsely chopped, drained
2 tsp minced thyme
Fresh ground pepper to taste
6 cups cooked rigatoni pasta

Garnish:
2 Tbsp grated Parmesan cheese

Monounsaturated Fat Exchange	1/2
Starch Exchange	2
Vegetable Exchange	2
Calories	232
Total Fat	4 g
Saturated Fat	1 g
Calories from Fat	35
Cholesterol	1 mg
Sodium	178 mg
Total Carbohydrate	41 g
Dietary Fiber	4 g
Sugars	6 g
Protein	8 g

1. In a heavy skillet over medium heat, heat the oil and wine together. Add the garlic and onion and saute for 5 minutes. Add the eggplant and saute for 5 more minutes.
2. Add the mushrooms and saute until mushrooms begin to brown, about 5 minutes. Add the plum tomatoes and bring to a boil. Lower the heat, cover, and simmer 10 minutes. Add the minced thyme and fresh ground pepper.
3. Toss the sauce with the cooked rigatoni. Top with Parmesan cheese.

Preparation time: 15 minutes

Shells Agli Olio

6 servings/serving size: 1 cup

This is the simplest of all Italian sauces.

1/4 cup olive oil
2 Tbsp white wine
10 garlic cloves, minced
1 cup fresh spinach leaves, stems
  removed, torn into small pieces
1 lb cooked shell pasta

Monounsaturated Fat Exchange	1 1/2
Starch Exchange	2 1/2
Calories	256
Total Fat	10 g
Saturated Fat	1 g
Calories from Fat	89
Cholesterol	0 mg
Sodium	10 mg
Total Carbohydrate	35 g
Dietary Fiber	2 g
Sugars	3 g
Protein	6 g

1. In a heavy skillet, heat the oil and wine. Add the garlic and saute for 5 minutes. Add the spinach and saute just until it wilts.
2. Toss the garlic spinach sauce with the hot shells and serve.

Preparation time: 8 minutes

We must use time as a tool, not as a couch.
—John Fitzgerald Kennedy

Angel Hair Pasta with Tomato Seafood Cream Sauce

6 servings/serving size: 1 cup with 2 oz seafood

Angel hair pasta is light and quick-cooking.

2 tsp olive oil
2 garlic cloves, minced
1 cup seeded, finely diced tomato
1 1/2 cups evaporated skim milk
1 tsp marjoram
Fresh ground pepper to taste
12 oz sea scallops
6 cups cooked angel hair pasta

Very Lean Meat	
Exchange	1
Starch Exchange	3
Calories	289
Total Fat	3 g
Saturated Fat	0 g
Calories from Fat	27
Cholesterol	21 mg
Sodium	169 mg
Total Carbohydrate ..	44 g
Dietary Fiber	2 g
Sugars	10 g
Protein	20 g

1. In a skillet over medium-high heat, heat the oil. Add the garlic and saute for 30 seconds. Add the tomato and saute for 2 minutes.
2. Add the evaporated milk and stir constantly over medium heat until thickened. Add the marjoram and pepper.
3. Add the scallops and cook for 2 minutes until the scallops turn opaque.
4. Pour the sauce over the angel hair pasta and serve.

Preparation time: 15 minutes

Moroccan Couscous with Chickpeas

6 servings/serving size: 1 cup

Using couscous is the fastest way to get a good main dish on the table in minutes. No stovetop is required—just rehydrate the couscous and eat!

Couscous:
2 cups dry couscous, rehydrated (To rehydrate, pour 4 cups boiling water over the couscous in a heat-proof bowl. Let stand for 5 minutes until the water is absorbed.)
1 cup canned chickpeas (garbonzo beans), drained
1/4 cup minced parsley
2 Tbsp minced scallions

Dressing:
1/4 cup fresh lemon juice
2 Tbsp olive oil
1 Tbsp cumin
1 tsp coriander
1 tsp paprika
1/2 tsp cayenne pepper
2 garlic cloves, minced

Starch Exchange	4
Calories	320
Total Fat	6 g
Saturated Fat	1 g
Calories from Fat	51
Cholesterol	0 mg
Sodium	50 mg
Total Carbohydrate	56 g
Dietary Fiber	5 g
Sugars	3 g
Protein	10 g

Preparation time: 10 minutes

1. In a bowl, combine the couscous, chickpeas, parsley, and scallions.
2. Combine all dressing ingredients and pour over the couscous and chickpeas. Serve at room temperature or refrigerate until ready to serve.

Couscous Tabouli

6 servings/serving size: 1 cup

Using couscous instead of the traditional grain, bulgur wheat, will save you some time—and the results are just as delicious!

Couscous:
1 1/2 cups dry couscous, rehydrated
(To rehydrate, pour 4 cups
boiling water over the couscous
in a heat-proof bowl. Let stand
for 5 minutes until the water is
absorbed.)
2 medium tomatoes, chopped
4 scallions, chopped
1/2 cup diced cucumber
1 cup minced parsley

Dressing:
1/4 cup lemon juice
2 Tbsp olive oil
1 tsp cumin
Fresh ground pepper and salt to taste

Monounsaturated Fat Exchange	1/2
Starch Exchange	2 1/2
Vegetable Exchange	1
Calories	233
Total Fat	5 g
Saturated Fat	1 g
Calories from Fat	46
Cholesterol	0 mg
Sodium	42 mg
Total Carbohydrate	40 g
Dietary Fiber	4 g
Sugars	3 g
Protein	7 g

1. Combine the rehydrated couscous with the tomatoes, scallions, cucumber, and parsley.
2. Whisk together the dressing ingredients.
3. Pour dressing over the couscous and serve, or refrigerate until serving time.

Preparation time: 15 minutes

Vegetable Rice and Beans

6 servings/serving size: 1 cup

This is a quick skillet dish to whip up with ingredients you probably have on hand. Precook white or brown rice to save time, and keep covered in a container in the refrigerator. Brown rice will take longer to cook, so cook a batch each week to use for easy dinners.

4 cups cooked white or brown rice
2 tsp olive oil
1 medium onion, chopped
3 cloves garlic, minced
2 medium tomatoes, finely diced
1 carrot, peeled and diced
1 15-oz can red kidney beans
1 tsp minced thyme
Fresh ground pepper to taste

Starch Exchange	3
Calories	248
Total Fat	3 g
Saturated Fat	1 g
Calories from Fat	29
Cholesterol	0 mg
Sodium	277 mg
Total Carbohydrate	48 g
Dietary Fiber	6 g
w/white rice	4 g
Sugars	6 g
Protein	8 g

1. In a heavy skillet over medium heat, heat the oil. Add the onion and garlic and saute for 5 minutes.
2. Add the tomatoes and carrot and cook for 5–8 more minutes. Add the kidney beans and thyme and simmer for 5 minutes. Grind in pepper.
3. Pour the vegetable bean mixture over hot cooked rice and serve.

Preparation time: 15 minutes

Indian Rice Curry

6 servings/serving size: 1 cup

Having cooked rice on hand means this aromatic dish can be ready fast.

2 tsp olive oil
1 small onion, minced
1/4 cup chopped tart apple
2 tsp curry powder
dash cayenne pepper
4 cups cooked white or brown rice
2 cups canned chickpeas, drained
1 Tbsp fresh lemon juice
Fresh ground pepper to taste

Starch Exchange	3
Calories	257
Total Fat	4 g
Saturated Fat	1 g
Calories from Fat	37
Cholesterol	0 mg
Sodium	86 mg
Total Carbohydrate	47 g
Dietary Fiber	5 g
w/white rice	3 g
Sugars	5 g
Protein	8 g

1. In a heavy skillet over medium heat, heat the oil. Add the onion and saute for 3 minutes. Add the apple and saute for 3 more minutes. Add the curry powder and cayenne to coat the apple and onion.
2. Add the cooked rice and chickpeas. Cook through until rice and beans are hot. Sprinkle with lemon juice and serve.

Preparation time: 10 minutes

Two-Tone Rice Pilaf

6 servings/serving size: 1 cup

Here, have the best of both worlds: fluffy white rice and nutty brown rice team up in this Italian-flavored dish.

2 tsp olive oil
1 medium onion, minced
4 garlic cloves, minced
2 scallions, minced
4 plum tomatoes, chopped
1 cup sliced asparagus
1/2 cup low-fat, low-sodium chicken broth
2 Tbsp fresh minced basil
1 tsp fresh minced oregano
1/2 cup sliced rehydrated sun-dried tomatoes
2 cups each cooked brown and white rice
Fresh ground pepper to taste

Starch Exchange....	2 1/2
Calories	203
Total Fat	3 g
Saturated Fat	1 g
Calories from Fat	27
Cholesterol	0 mg
Sodium	99 mg
Total Carbohydrate	40 g
Dietary Fiber	4 g
Sugars	5 g
Protein	6 g

1. In a heavy skillet, heat the oil. Add the onion and garlic and saute for 5 minutes. Add the scallions and saute 1 minute.
2. Add the tomatoes, asparagus, and chicken broth. Cover the pan and let steam for 3–4 minutes.
3. Add the basil, oregano, and sun-dried tomatoes. Simmer for 5 minutes.
4. Add the cooked rices and toss well. Serve.

Preparation time: 15 minutes

The Daily Catch

Most people probably have fond memories of the only fish dish they ate as children: breaded frozen fishsticks! Today there are so many varieties of fresh fish it is hard to resist preparing it in new and delicious ways.

Here are a few pointers on selecting your fish:

☞ Try to go to a fish market that you are familiar with. This way you will know their delivery schedule and can be assured of the freshest fish possible.

☞ Look for steaks and fillets that appear to be freshly cut without a dried or brown look. A mushy flesh may indicate that the fish has been defrosted and refrozen.

☞ Plan your menus carefully. Fresh fish should be used within 24 hours for the best taste and freshness. Keep fresh fish on ice in your refrigerator to keep it at its best. If you must freeze your fish, wrap the fish well and try to use it within 1–3 months.

☞ Be gentle when you cook fish! Fish is done when it just turns opaque. If it overflakes, it is overcooked! When cooking shellfish like shrimp, cook it just until it turns pink, then remove it from the heat source. Scallops should be cooked just until they turn opaque, about 1–2 minutes.

Put the bait on, throw the line—it's time for some great fish!

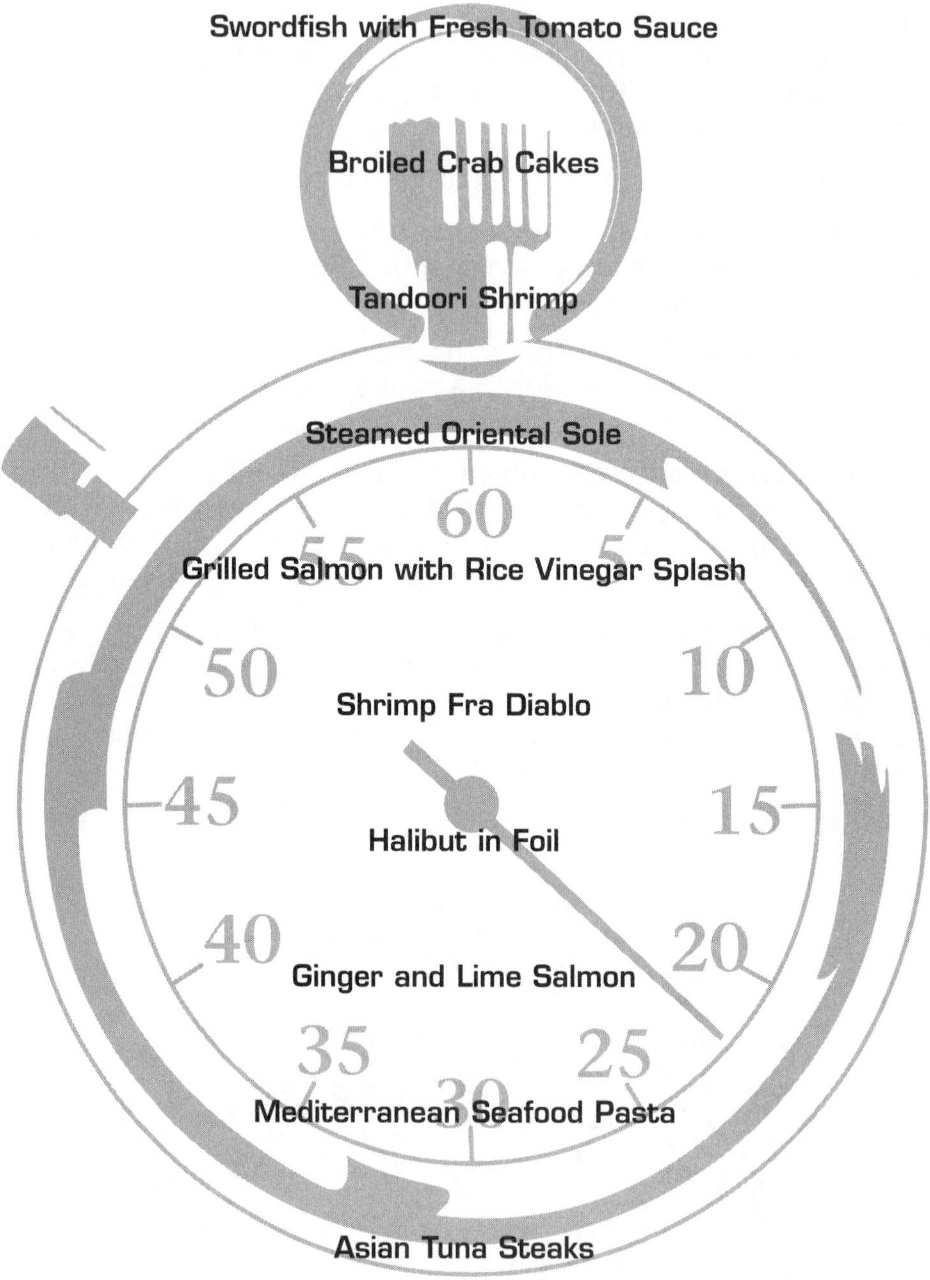

Swordfish with Fresh Tomato Sauce

Broiled Crab Cakes

Tandoori Shrimp

Steamed Oriental Sole

Grilled Salmon with Rice Vinegar Splash

Shrimp Fra Diablo

Halibut in Foil

Ginger and Lime Salmon

Mediterranean Seafood Pasta

Asian Tuna Steaks

Swordfish with Fresh Tomato Sauce

6 servings/serving size: 3 oz fish and sauce

Keep swordfish juicy and moist with this fresh-from-the-vine tomato sauce.

Fish:
1 1/2 lb swordfish steaks
2 Tbsp fresh lemon juice
1 Tbsp olive oil

Sauce:
1/4 cup white wine
4 ripe tomatoes, chopped
3 garlic cloves, minced
2 scallions, chopped
2 tsp minced thyme

Very Lean Meat Exchange	3
Vegetable Exchange	1
Fat Exchange	1
Calories	178
Total Fat	6 g
Saturated Fat	1 g
Calories from Fat	54
Cholesterol	44 mg
Sodium	113 mg
Total Carbohydrate	6 g
Dietary Fiber	1 g
Sugars	4 g
Protein	23 g

1. Marinate the fish in the lemon juice and olive oil for 10 minutes at room temperature while you prepare the tomato sauce.
2. In a heavy skillet, heat the wine. When it is slightly boiling, add the garlic and scallions. Saute for 3 minutes. Add the tomatoes and thyme. Bring to a boil and simmer for 5 minutes.
3. Remove the swordfish from the marinade. Grill or broil the swordfish for 3–4 minutes per side. Top with the fresh tomato sauce to serve.

Preparation time: 10 minutes

Broiled Crab Cakes

6 servings/serving size: 3 oz

Nothing hits the spot like a simple broiled crab cake.

1 1/2 lb backfin crabmeat, cartilage
    and shells removed
2 Tbsp low-fat mayonnaise
2 Tbsp Dijon mustard
3 Tbsp minced onion
1 egg
Dash Tabasco sauce

Very Lean Meat	
Exchange	3
Fat Exchange	1/2
Calories	131
Total Fat	4 g
Saturated Fat	1 g
Calories from Fat	38
Cholesterol	132 mg
Sodium	375 mg
Total Carbohydrate	1 g
Dietary Fiber	0 g
Sugars	1 g
Protein	20 g

Combine all ingredients and shape into 6 patties. Broil 6 inches from heat source, 3 minutes per side, until golden brown. Serve immediately.

I've been on a calendar, but never on time.
—Marilyn Monroe

Tandoori Shrimp

6 servings/serving size: 4 oz

Although this shrimp must marinate for several hours, the rest of the preparation is a breeze.

3 Tbsp coarsely chopped ginger
1 medium onion, coarsely chopped
6 garlic cloves
1/4 cup olive oil
1 1/4 cup plain low- or nonfat yogurt
2 Tbsp ground cumin
1 tsp turmeric
2 tsp paprika
1 tsp cayenne pepper
1 1/2 lb shelled and deveined large
    shrimp

Lean Meat Exchange	3
Calories	172
Total Fat	7 g
Saturated Fat	1 g
Calories from Fat	60
Cholesterol	171 mg
Sodium	175 mg
Total Carbohydrate	3 g
Dietary Fiber	0 g
Sugars	3 g
Protein	24 g

1. Combine all marinade ingredients in a food processor or blender. Marinate the shrimp for 4 hours.
2. Grill the shrimp for 3 minutes 6 inches from the heat source.

Preparation time: 10 minutes

Steamed Oriental Sole

6 servings/serving size: 3 oz

This fish has an elegant flavor, but is simple to prepare.

2 scallions, cut diagonally into 1-inch
  pieces
2 carrots, peeled and julienned
1 cup finely chopped bok choy
  cabbage
1 cup fresh snow peas, trimmed
4 thin slices fresh ginger, julienned
1 1/2 lb sole fillets
3 Tbsp lite soy sauce
1 Tbsp sesame oil
2 Tbsp dry sherry

Very Lean Meat Exchange	3
Fat Exchange	1/2
Vegetable Exchange	1
Calories	164
Total Fat	4 g
Saturated Fat	1 g
Calories from Fat	33
Cholesterol	60 mg
Sodium	429 mg
Total Carbohydrate	8 g
Dietary Fiber	2 g
Sugars	4 g
Protein	23 g

1. Prepare the vegetables. Place the sole fillets on a large heat-proof plate. Scatter all the vegetables over the sole fillets.
2. Combine the soy sauce, sesame oil, and sherry. Sprinkle the sauce over the vegetables and fish.
3. Place a steamer rack in a large wok or saucepot. Pour 3 inches of water into the bottom of the wok or pot. Place the plate of fish and vegetables on the steamer rack.
4. Cover and let steam on high heat for 5–8 minutes. Add more water to the bottom of the wok or pot if necessary. Remove fish and vegetables and serve.

Preparation time: 10 minutes

Grilled Salmon with Rice Vinegar Splash

6 servings/serving size: 3 oz

The secret to this dish is splashing a very simple rice vinegar sauce on the salmon fillets just after you remove them from the broiler.

Salmon:
1 1/2 lb salmon fillets
1 Tbsp olive oil

Sauce:
1 cup rice vinegar
3 cloves garlic, minced
3 shallots, finely minced
3 slices ginger, minced

Garnish:
Sprigs of parsley or cilantro

Monounsaturated Fat Exchange	1/2
Lean Meat Exchange	3
Vegetable Exchange	1
Calories	220
Total Fat	12 g
Saturated Fat	2 g
Calories from Fat	108
Cholesterol	77 mg
Sodium	60 mg
Total Carbohydrate	3 g
Dietary Fiber	0 g
Sugars	2 g
Protein	24 g

1. Combine all sauce ingredients and set aside.
2. Brush each salmon fillet with a little olive oil. Broil 6 inches from the heat source for 3–4 minutes per side until done.
3. Splash the sauce over the cooked salmon fillets. Garnish with parsley or cilantro.

Preparation time: 10 minutes

Shrimp Fra Diablo

6 servings/serving size: 3 oz shrimp plus sauce

"Fra Diablo" means a spicy tomato sauce. Serve this dish with pasta to cool it off a bit.

1 Tbsp olive oil
3 garlic cloves, minced
1 medium onion, chopped
1 15-oz can tomato puree
1 6-oz can tomato paste
2 Tbsp red wine
2 tsp crushed red pepper
2 tsp capers
2 Tbsp minced basil
1 1/2 lb shelled and deveined medium
   shrimp

Very Lean Meat	
Exchange	3
Starch Exchange	1
Calories	205
Total Fat	5 g
Saturated Fat	1 g
Calories from Fat	42
Cholesterol	170 mg
Sodium	299 mg
Total Carbohydrate	16 g
Dietary Fiber	3 g
Sugars	8 g
Protein	25 g

1. In a heavy skillet, heat the oil. Add the garlic and onion and saute for 5 minutes. Add the tomato puree and tomato paste. Bring to a boil.
2. Add the red wine, red pepper, and capers. Lower the heat and simmer for 15 minutes.
3. Add the shrimp and cook over low heat for 4–5 minutes until shrimp just turn pink. Serve over pasta if desired.

Preparation time: 15 minutes

Halibut in Foil

6 servings/serving size: 3–4 oz

This French method of preparing fish ensures a moist, tender fillet every time.

2 tsp olive oil
6 4-oz halibut steaks
1/2 cup dry white wine
6 thyme sprigs
6 thin lemon slices
1 1/2 tsp fennel seeds
6 parsley sprigs
Fresh ground pepper to taste

Very Lean Meat	
Exchange	4
Calories	144
Total Fat	4 g
Saturated Fat	1 g
Calories from Fat	37
Cholesterol	36 mg
Sodium	62 mg
Total Carbohydrate	0 g
Dietary Fiber	0 g
Sugars	0 g
Protein	24 g

1. Preheat the oven to 350 degrees. Tear aluminum foil into 6 large squares. Brush each square with some olive oil.
2. Place the halibut in the center of the square. Drizzle each steak with some of the wine. Put a thyme sprig, lemon slices, a few fennel seeds, and a parsley sprig on each piece of fish.
3. Grind pepper over each piece of fish. Seal the foil into a packet. Place all packets on a baking sheet and bake for 10–15 minutes. Place a packet on each plate and let each person carefully open the packet. Pour all juices on top of the fish.

Preparation time: 10 minutes

Ginger and Lime Salmon

6 servings/serving size: 3 oz

Salmon does not need any special preparation. In fact, it is best just enhanced with a few flavorful ingredients.

1 Tbsp sesame oil
1 Tbsp lite soy sauce
1 Tbsp grated ginger
2 Tbsp dry sherry
6 4-oz salmon fillets
1 Tbsp grated lime peel
1 Tbsp minced scallions
12 lime wedges

Monounsaturated Fat Exchange	1/2
Lean Meat Exchange	3
Calories	205
Total Fat	11 g
Saturated Fat	2 g
Calories from Fat	98
Cholesterol	77 mg
Sodium	109 mg
Total Carbohydrate	1 g
Dietary Fiber	0 g
Sugars	0 g
Protein	24 g

1. Mix together the sesame oil, soy sauce, ginger, and sherry. Sprinkle over the salmon and let it marinate for 15 minutes.
2. Prepare to steam. Fill the bottom of a large wok or saucepot with 3 inches of water. Place a steamer rack in the wok or pot. Place the fish fillets on a heat-proof plate. Cover the wok or pot and steam the fish for 10 minutes, until it is tender.
3. Sprinkle the fish with lime peel and scallions. Serve with lime wedges.

Preparation time: 10 minutes

Mediterranean Seafood Pasta

6 servings/serving size: 1 cup cooked pasta with 3 1/2 oz seafood

Fruits of the sea enliven this European-inspired dish.

2 tsp olive oil
1 medium onion, minced
1 medium carrot, diced
1/2 cup each diced red and green peppers
1 1/2 cups crushed canned tomatoes
3 Tbsp dry white wine
2 tsp dried oregano
1 tsp dried or fresh chopped thyme
2 Tbsp lemon juice
1 lb shelled and deveined medium shrimp
1/2 lb sea scallops
6 cups cooked, shaped pasta (use rigatoni, penne, or shells)

Very Lean Meat	
Exchange	2
Starch Exchange	3
Calories	315
Total Fat	3 g
Saturated Fat	1 g
Calories from Fat	31
Cholesterol	125 mg
Sodium	386 mg
Total Carbohydrate	43 g
Dietary Fiber	4 g
Sugars	7 g
Protein	26 g

1. In a large skillet, heat the oil. Add the onion and carrot and saute for 5 minutes. Add the peppers and saute for 3 more minutes.
2. Add the crushed tomatoes, wine, oregano, thyme, and lemon juice. Bring to a boil. Simmer for 10 minutes.
3. Add the seafood and cook over medium heat for 5 minutes until shrimp have turned pink and scallops are no longer translucent.
4. Place 3 1/2 oz of the seafood and sauce over each serving of pasta.

Preparation time: 15 minutes

Asian Tuna Steaks

6 servings/serving size: 3–4 oz

Serve these tender steaks with Broccoli Salad (see p. 47) for a delicious meal.

Tuna:
1 1/2 lb tuna steaks

Marinade:
1/4 cup orange juice (fresh or frozen)
2 Tbsp sesame oil
2 tsp sesame seeds
3 Tbsp lite soy sauce
1 Tbsp fresh grated ginger (or use 2 tsp ground ginger)
3 Tbsp chopped scallions

Lean Meat Exchange	3
Calories	184
Total Fat	8 g
Saturated Fat	2 g
Calories from Fat	71
Cholesterol	42
Sodium	194 mg
Total Carbohydrate	1 g
Dietary Fiber	0 g
Sugars	1 g
Protein	26 g

1. In a stainless steel bowl or plastic ziploc bag, combine all ingredients. Add the tuna and let marinate for 20 minutes.
2. Broil or grill the tuna 6 inches from the heat source for 4 to 5 minutes per side. Cook until done as desired (some people prefer their tuna more rare than others do).

Preparation time: 10 minutes

Perfect Poultry

Poultry is a great low-fat, high-protein food choice! Stick with white meat of chicken and breast of turkey—dark meat of chicken and turkey, as well as any part of goose and duck, are too high in fat and should be reserved for special occasions. Whole chickens and Cornish game hens are delicious, but can take a long time to prepare. You might enjoy free-range chicken—it's more expensive, but the meat is even lower in fat than regular chicken and has a tender, delicious flavor. Try to buy ground turkey from a butcher that grinds his own meat—most commercially prepared ground turkey contains a lot of dark meat and skin.

The first step in creating juicy, mouth-watering recipes is to always buy chicken and turkey with the skin attached. This fat layer keeps the cut of meat moist, and makes the final product juicier. You should still remove the skin from the meat before cooking it—3 ounces of chicken skin has 40 grams of fat! It's easy to make tasty chicken by marinating it. Marinating ensures that the tougher meat fibers are broken down, and yields juicy, tender meat. Cooking chicken quickly also helps ensure tenderness.

South-of-The-Border Chicken with Variations

"Wok" This Way

Chicken Stir-Fry with Vegetables

Crunchy Chicken with Asparagus

Spicy Chicken with Peppers

Southwestern Chicken Salad

Curried Chicken Salad with Grapes

Chicken Tarragon Salad

Chicken and Grapes

Bombay Chicken

Chicken Paprikash

Chicken Marsala

Turkey Burritos

Grilled Turkey with Garlic Sauce

Turkey Provençal

Stuffed Zucchini Boats

South-of-The-Border Chicken with Variations

6 servings/serving size: 3–4 oz

This recipe provides several different marinades so you can cook variations of this delicious dish. (See pages 84–85 for microwave directions and marinade variations.)

Chicken:
3 whole chicken breasts, skinned, boned, and halved

Marinade:
1/2 cup fresh lime juice
1 Tbsp olive oil
1/2 cup chopped yellow onion
1/2 cup chopped red pepper
2 garlic cloves, minced
2 Tbsp minced cilantro
1 Tbsp fresh minced oregano (or 1 tsp dried oregano)

Garnish:
Lime slices

Very Lean Meat	
Exchange	4
Calories	155
Total Fat	4 g
Saturated Fat	1 g
Calories from Fat	38
Cholesterol	73 mg
Sodium	64 mg
Total Carbohydrate	1 g
Dietary Fiber	0 g
Sugars	0 g
Protein	27 g

1. In a large bowl, combine all marinade ingredients. Add the chicken breasts and marinate for at least 2–3 hours, or up to two days.
2. To cook, drain marinade. Add the chicken breast halves to a broiler pan and set the oven rack 6 inches from the heat source, or place the chicken on a hot outside grill with the grill rack set 6 inches above the heat source. Grill the chicken for 7–8 minutes per side until no trace of pink remains.
3. Garnish with lime slices and serve.

Marinade Variations

Follow the above directions for South-of-The-Border Chicken, except try one of these different marinades. All of these marinades will coat enough for 3 whole chicken breasts (about 21–23 oz). All marinades have the same nutritional analysis except the Rice Vinegar marinade, which has 116 mg of sodium.

Balsamic Mustard
1/4 cup low-fat, low-sodium chicken broth
2 garlic cloves, minced
1/2 cup balsamic vinegar
3 Tbsp Dijon mustard
1 Tbsp olive oil
1 Tbsp minced scallions

Herb Marinade
2 Tbsp minced parsley
2 tsp fresh minced thyme
2 tsp fresh rosemary
2 sage leaves
1 tsp fresh minced tarragon
1/3 cup sherry vinegar
1 Tbsp olive oil
Fresh ground pepper to taste

Rice Vinegar
1/2 cup rice vinegar
2 Tbsp dry sherry
1 Tbsp sesame oil
3 garlic cloves, minced
1 Tbsp lite soy sauce
Ground white pepper

Orange Cumin
1/4 cup fresh orange juice
1 Tbsp olive oil
2 tsp grated orange peel
1 tsp cumin
2 tsp minced parsley
2 Tbsp white wine

Lemon Pepper
1/2 cup dry white wine
1 Tbsp olive oil
1/3 cup low-fat, low-sodium chicken broth
1/4 cup lemon juice
2 tsp grated lemon peel
1 garlic clove, minced
1 Tbsp whole black peppercorns

Raspberry Shallot
1/2 cup raspberry vinegar
1 Tbsp olive oil
3 Tbsp minced shallots
2 tsp minced thyme
Fresh ground pepper to taste

Microwave directions:
If you prefer to microwave your chicken, marinate the chicken
as above. Arrange the chicken on a trivet in a baking dish big
enough to accommodate all the chicken. Put the meatier
portions facing the walls of the microwave. Cover the chicken
with waxed paper and cook on full power (high) for about 14
minutes until juices run clear. Let stand for 4 minutes, covered.
Garnish with lime slices.

"Wok" This Way

Using a wok can help you get dinner on the table fast. Here are some tips for fool-proof wok cooking and several easy, delicious recipes to make.

☞ There are many woks to choose from. Buy one that suits your needs. It is preferable to purchase a non-electric wok. Woks created for the stove tend to be deeper and are better made than electric woks.

☞ Season your wok well. A properly seasoned wok will provide many years of cooking pleasure. Read the manufacturer's directions carefully for correct seasoning.

☞ Your stirring spoon should be long-handled and preferably have a flat edge. This will help with the fast hand motion necessary to stir-fry properly.

☞ Heat your wok without anything in it just a few seconds prior to beginning the recipe. This will prevent food from sticking to the wok.

☞ When adding food to the wok, make sure your ingredients are not ice-cold. Bring meat, poultry, and fish up to room temperature prior to placing them in the wok. Otherwise, food will stick to the wok.

☞ Assemble all your ingredients first and then proceed to stir-fry. Stir-frying is a very quick process and all ingredients need to be washed, chopped, and sliced so they are ready to go.

Chicken Stir-Fry with Vegetables

6 servings/serving size: 1 cup with 3 oz chicken

No oil is used to prepare this extremely tender chicken.

3 chicken breasts, halved, boned, and skinned
1 egg white, beaten
1 Tbsp cornstarch or arrowroot powder
3 Tbsp low-fat, low-sodium chicken broth
1/2 cup sliced mushrooms
2 small zucchini, cut into strips, unpeeled
1 cup fresh snow peas, trimmed
1/2 cup sliced scallions
1 Tbsp lite soy sauce

Very Lean Meat Exchange	4
Vegetable Exchange	1
Calories	171
Total Fat	3 g
Saturated Fat	1 g
Calories from Fat	29
Cholesterol	73 mg
Sodium	180 mg
Total Carbohydrate	5 g
Dietary Fiber	2 g
Sugars	2 g
Protein	29 g

1. Flatten each breast of chicken by placing it between two pieces of waxed paper and pounding it with a meat mallet. Pound until the breast is 1/4 inch thick. Cut into bite-size pieces.
2. Place chicken in a bowl. Add the egg white and cornstarch or arrowroot powder. Stir thoroughly. Let the chicken sit for 10 minutes and prepare all the vegetables.
3. Heat the broth in the wok. Add the chicken and stir-fry until it turns opaque, about 5–6 minutes. Remove the chicken from the wok.
4. Add the mushrooms to the wok and stir-fry for 2 minutes. Add the zucchini, snow peas, scallions, and soy sauce. Cover the pan and steam for 2 minutes. Add the chicken back to the wok and steam 1 more minute.

Preparation time: 15 minutes

Crunchy Chicken with Asparagus

6 servings/serving size: 1 cup with 3–4 oz chicken

The asparagus in this dish should remain bright green. Asparagus is best when it is crisp.

2 tsp peanut oil
2 Tbsp low-fat, low-sodium chicken broth
3 cloves garlic, minced
2 Tbsp minced scallions
3 chicken breasts, boned, skinned, halved, and cubed into 2-inch pieces
1 medium carrot, sliced thin
2 cups sliced asparagus (slice into 2-inch pieces)
1/2 cup water chestnuts
2 Tbsp lite soy sauce
2 Tbsp white wine vinegar
1 tsp sesame oil
1/4 cup low-fat, low-sodium chicken broth
1 Tbsp cornstarch or arrowroot powder

Very Lean Meat Exchange	4
Vegetable Exchange	1
Fat Exchange	1/2
Calories	200
Total Fat	6 g
Saturated Fat	1 g
Calories from Fat	51
Cholesterol	73 mg
Sodium	289 mg
Total Carbohydrate	8 g
Dietary Fiber	2 g
Sugars	3 g
Protein	29 g

Preparation time: 15 minutes

1. In a wok over medium-high heat, heat the oil and broth. Add the garlic and scallions and saute for 30 seconds. Add the chicken and stir-fry for 5–8 minutes until it is opaque.
2. Push the chicken up on the sides of the wok. Add a little broth, if necessary, and add the carrot. Stir-fry for 2 minutes. Add the asparagus and stir-fry for 3 minutes. Add the water chestnuts and stir-fry 2 more minutes. Add chicken back to the center of the wok.
3. Combine the last five ingredients and mix until smooth. Add the sauce to the wok. Stir, cover, and steam for 2 minutes.

Spicy Chicken with Peppers

6 servings/serving size: 1 cup (3 oz chicken)

This dish is not for the fainthearted. However, use fewer chili peppers if you want to tone the flavor down a bit.

1 Tbsp peanut oil
3 garlic cloves, minced
3 small red chili peppers, minced
3 chicken breasts, boned, skinned, halved, and cut into 2-inch pieces
2 Tbsp low-fat, low-sodium chicken broth
1 each small red and green pepper, sliced thin
1 cup sliced celery
1/2 cup sliced scallions
1 Tbsp lite soy sauce

Very Lean Meat Exchange	4
Vegetable Exchange	1
Fat Exchange	1/2
Calories	190
Total Fat	6 g
Saturated Fat	1 g
Calories from Fat	50
Cholesterol	73 mg
Sodium	185 mg
Total Carbohydrate	7 g
Dietary Fiber	1 g
Sugars	3 g
Protein	28 g

1. In a wok, heat the oil over medium-high heat. Add the garlic and chili peppers and stir-fry for 30 seconds. Do not let the mixture burn.
2. Add the chicken and stir-fry for 5–8 minutes until it is opaque. Push the chicken up on the sides of the wok.
3. Add the chicken broth to the wok. Stir-fry the peppers for 4 minutes. Add the celery and scallions and stir-fry for 2 minutes.
4. Push the chicken back to the center of the wok. Add the soy sauce. Cover and steam for 2 minutes.

Preparation time: 15 minutes

Southwestern Chicken Salad

6 servings/serving size: 1 cup

You could also omit the chicken from this recipe for a high-fiber, vegetarian bean and corn salad (the nutritional analysis is in parentheses; the yield is 4 1-cup servings).

Salad:

1 cup cooked corn kernels
1 cup diced tomatoes
1 cup green peas, frozen and thawed
1/2 cup each sliced red and green pepper
1/3 cup canned black beans, drained
2 cups cooked, cubed chicken breast

Dressing:

1 Tbsp olive oil
1/4 cup lime juice
2 tsp cumin
1 Tbsp chopped cilantro
2 tsp chili powder
1 tsp oregano

Very Lean Meat Exchange	2 (0)
Monounsaturated Fat Exchange	1/2 (1/2)
Starch Exchange	1 (1 1/2)
Calories	181 (137)
Total Fat	6 g (4 g)
Saturated Fat	1 g (1 g)
Calories from Fat	55 (36)
Cholesterol	42 mg (0 mg)
Sodium	94 mg (80 mg)
Total Carbohydrate	16 g (23 g)
Dietary Fiber	4 g (6 g)
Sugars	4 g (6 g)
Protein	17 g (5 g)

Combine all salad ingredients. In a blender or food processor, blend all dressing ingredients. Toss the dressing with the salad and serve.

Preparation time: 10 minutes

Curried Chicken Salad with Grapes

6 servings/serving size: 1 cup

This is a creamy smooth salad with a hint of curry.

Salad:
3 cups cooked, cubed chicken breasts
1 1/2 cups halved green or red grapes
1/2 cup sliced celery
2 Tbsp sliced scallions
1/2 cup diced red pepper

Dressing:
3/4 cup low-fat mayonnaise
2 Tbsp orange juice
1 tsp curry powder
Fresh ground pepper to taste

Lean Meat Exchange	4
Starch Exchange	1/2
Calories	273
Total Fat	12 g
Saturated Fat	2 g
Calories from Fat	112
Cholesterol	84 mg
Sodium	293 mg
Total Carbohydrate	10 g
Dietary Fiber	1 g
Sugars	8 g
Protein	27 g

Combine all salad ingredients. Combine all dressing ingredients in a small bowl and whisk together until smooth. Toss the dressing with the salad and serve.

Preparation time: 10 minutes

You will never "find" time for anything.
If you want time, you must make it.
—Charles Brixton

Chicken Tarragon Salad

6 servings/serving size: 1 cup

Cook up a whole chicken or some breasts to keep on hand for making chicken salads. This recipe and the following two are more interesting than a basic chicken salad. For a fresh-tasting salad, use cooked chicken that has been in your refrigerator for just 2 or 3 days.

Salad:
3 cups cooked, cubed chicken breast
1 cup sliced celery
1 cup diced onion
1/2 cup diced zucchini, unpeeled

Dressing:
3/4 cup low-fat mayonnaise
2 Tbsp low-fat sour cream
2 Tbsp minced tarragon
1 Tbsp minced parsley
Fresh ground pepper to taste

Lean Meat Exchange	4
Starch Exchange	1/2
Calories	261
Total Fat	13 g
Saturated Fat	3 g
Calories from Fat	115
Cholesterol	86 mg
Sodium	305 mg
Total Carbohydrate	5 g
Dietary Fiber	1 g
Sugars	4 g
Protein	27 g

Combine all salad ingredients. Combine all dressing ingredients in a small bowl and whisk together until smooth. Toss the dressing with the salad and serve.

Preparation time: 10 minutes

Chicken and Grapes

6 servings/serving size: 3–4 oz

This is the French-inspired recipe Chicken Veronique, without the cream or butter.

3 whole chicken breasts, boned, skinned, and halved, pounded to 1/4-inch thickness
1/3 cup unbleached white flour
Fresh ground pepper and salt to taste
2 tsp canola oil
1 small onion, minced
1 cup low-fat, low-sodium chicken broth
3 Tbsp low-sugar orange marmalade
2 tsp fresh minced rosemary
2 tsp lemon juice
1 1/2 cups halved green grapes
1 Tbsp cornstarch or arrowroot powder
2 Tbsp water
Fresh ground pepper to taste

Very Lean Meat Exchange	4
Starch Exchange	1
Calories	**234**
Total Fat	**5 g**
Saturated Fat	1 g
Calories from Fat	48
Cholesterol	**73 mg**
Sodium	**112 mg**
Total Carbohydrate	**18 g**
Dietary Fiber	1 g
Sugars	9 g
Protein	**28 g**

Preparation time: 15 minutes

1. In a ziploc bag, combine the chicken breasts with the flour, salt, and pepper. Shake well.
2. In a large skillet over medium-high heat, heat the oil. Add the chicken breasts and saute on each side for 5 minutes. Remove the chicken from the skillet.
3. In the same skillet, saute the onion in the remaining pan drippings. Add the chicken broth and orange marmalade. Stir well. Add the rosemary and lemon juice and cook for 3 minutes. Add the grapes and cook for 5 minutes. Add the chicken back to the skillet and cook for 10 more minutes.
4. In a small measuring cup, combine the cornstarch or arrowroot powder with the water. Add to the skillet and cook until sauce is thickened. Add pepper to taste.

Bombay Chicken

6 servings/serving size: 3–4 oz

From the towers of the Taj Mahal, a dish fit for a king.

2 tsp corn oil
1 medium onion, minced
2 garlic cloves, minced
1 1/2 lb chicken breasts, boned, skinned, halved, and cut into 2-inch pieces
1 Tbsp curry powder
1 cup diagonally sliced carrots
1 cup cauliflower florets
1 1/2 cups evaporated skim milk
1/2 cup canned chickpeas, drained
1/4 cup raisins
1/2 cup frozen peas, thawed and drained
1 Tbsp cornstarch or arrowroot powder
2 Tbsp water

Very Lean Meat Exchange	4
Starch Exchange	1 1/2
Vegetable Exchange	1
Calories	**280**
Total Fat	**5 g**
Saturated Fat	1 g
Calories from Fat	48
Cholesterol	**71 mg**
Sodium	**185 mg**
Total Carbohydrate	**25 g**
Dietary Fiber	3 g
Sugars	14 g
Protein	**33 g**

1. Heat the oil in a large saucepot over medium-high heat. Add the onion, garlic, and chicken and saute until the chicken is almost cooked through, abut 5 minutes. Add the curry powder and cook for 3 more minutes.

Preparation time: 15 minutes

2. Place the carrots and cauliflower together on a steamer and steam over boiling water for 5–6 minutes. Remove from the heat and add to the chicken. Add the evaporated milk and cook for 5 minutes over medium heat.

3. Add the chickpeas, raisins, and peas. Mix together the cornstarch or arrowroot powder with the water. Add to the chicken mixture. Cook until sauce is thickened, about 3–5 minutes.

Chicken Paprikash

6 servings/serving size: 3–4 oz

This is a lighter version of the Hungarian favorite, made with low-fat sour cream.

2 tsp canola oil
1 medium onion, diced
3 whole chicken breasts, halved, boned, and skinned
1/2 cup low-fat, low-sodium chicken broth
2 Tbsp paprika
1 cup low-fat sour cream
Fresh ground pepper and salt to taste

Very Lean Meat Exchange	4
Starch Exchange	1/2
Fat Exchange	1
Calories	213
Total Fat	8 g
Saturated Fat	3 g
Calories from Fat	74
Cholesterol	86 mg
Sodium	115 mg
Total Carbohydrate	5 g
Dietary Fiber	1 g
Sugars	4 g
Protein	28 g

1. In a skillet over medium-high heat, heat the oil. Add the onion and saute for 5 minutes.
2. In a ziploc bag, shake the chicken breasts with 1 Tbsp of the paprika. Cook the chicken on each side until browned, about 5 minutes. Add the chicken broth to the skillet, bring to a boil, lower the heat, and cover for 10 minutes.
3. When broth has evaporated, remove the chicken from the skillet. Add the sour cream, remaining paprika, pepper, and salt. Heat over low heat for 2 minutes. Add the chicken breasts. Serve over hot noodles if desired.

Preparation time: 10 minutes

Chicken Marsala

6 servings/serving size: 3–4 oz

Every cook needs a good Italian chicken marsala recipe.

2 tsp olive oil
1 medium onion, chopped
1 1/2 lb whole chicken breasts, halved,
　　boned, and skinned, pounded to
　　1/4-inch thickness
1 cup dry marsala wine
3/4 cup low-fat, low-sodium chicken
　　broth
1 Tbsp cornstarch or arrowroot powder
Fresh ground pepper and salt to taste

Very Lean Meat	
Exchange	4
Starch Exchange	1/2
Calories	182
Total Fat	5 g
Saturated Fat	1 g
Calories from Fat	43
Cholesterol	69 mg
Sodium	99 mg
Total Carbohydrate	4 g
Dietary Fiber	0 g
Sugars	2 g
Protein	26 g

1. In a large skillet over medium-high heat, heat the oil. Add the onion and saute for 5 minutes. Add the chicken and cook on each side for 5 minutes.
2. Add the wine and cook for about 4 minutes until the wine looks syrupy.
3. In a small cup, dissolve the cornstarch or arrowroot powder in the broth. Add to the chicken and cook until the sauce is thickened, about 2 minutes. Add pepper and salt to taste.

Preparation time: 10 minutes

Turkey Burritos

6 servings/serving size: 3–4 oz in 1 6-inch tortilla

Turkey breast is just as easy to use as chicken breast, and adds great flavor to these burritos!

2 tsp olive oil
1 medium onion, chopped
2 garlic cloves, minced
1/2 cup diced green peppers
1 Tbsp chili powder
1 1/2 lb ground lean turkey breast
1 cup diced tomatoes
1/2 cup corn kernels
6 6-inch tortillas, heated (To heat: wrap in foil and place in a 300-degree oven until warm and soft, or wrap 3 tortillas in 2 damp paper towels and microwave on high for 1 minute.)
1 cup salsa

Very Lean Meat Exchange	4
Starch Exchange	1 1/2
Vegetable Exchange	1
Calories	274
Total Fat	5 g
Saturated Fat	1 g
Calories from Fat	41
Cholesterol	75 mg
Sodium	367 mg
Total Carbohydrate	26 g
Dietary Fiber	3 g
Sugars	6 g
Protein	32 g

1. In a skillet over medium-high heat, heat the oil. Add the onion and garlic and saute for 5 minutes. Add the peppers and saute for 3 more minutes.
2. Add the chili powder and ground turkey and saute until the turkey is no longer pink. Add the tomatoes and corn and cook 2 more minutes.
3. Spoon some of the turkey mixture into each warm tortilla. Roll up. Serve each tortilla with 2 Tbsp of salsa.

Preparation time: 15 minutes

Grilled Turkey with Garlic Sauce

6 servings/serving size: 3–4 oz with 2–3 Tbsp sauce

You can also use this sauce to top chicken.

1/3 cup minced parsley
5 garlic cloves, minced
1/3 cup lemon juice
1/4 cup olive oil
1 tsp paprika
1 tsp cumin
Dash cayenne pepper
1 1/2 lb turkey breast slices, pounded
    to 1/4-inch thickness
1 Tbsp olive oil for brushing on turkey
  while grilling

Lean Meat Exchange	4
Calories	229
Total Fat	12 g
Saturated Fat	2 g
Calories from Fat	108
Cholesterol	75 mg
Sodium	52 mg
Total Carbohydrate	2 g
Dietary Fiber	0 g
Sugars	1 g
Protein	28 g

1. In a blender, blend all sauce ingredients together.
2. Grill or broil the turkey breasts 6 inches from the heat source, brushing with olive oil to keep moist. Grill on each side about 4 minutes.
3. Top each slice with some of the sauce (about 2–3 Tbsp per slice).

Preparation time: 10 minutes

Turkey Provençal

6 servings/serving size: 3–4 oz

The delicious smell of this dish will draw an audience to your kitchen!

1 1/2 lb turkey fillets
2 Tbsp unbleached white flour
Fresh ground pepper and salt to taste
2 tsp olive oil
1 medium onion, diced
2 garlic cloves, minced
1 1/2 cups crushed canned tomatoes
1 tsp minced rosemary
1 Tbsp fresh chopped thyme
1/4 cup sliced black olives
2 tsp capers
1/2 cup minced parsley

Very Lean Meat Exchange	4
Vegetable Exchange	2
Calories	189
Total Fat	3 g
Saturated Fat	1 g
Calories from Fat	27
Cholesterol	75 mg
Sodium	294 mg
Total Carbohydrate	10 g
Dietary Fiber	2 g
Sugars	5 g
Protein	29 g

1. In a ziploc bag, place the turkey fillets with the flour, salt, and pepper. Shake the bag until the turkey fillets are coated with flour.
2. In a large skillet over medium heat, heat the oil. Add the turkey fillets and saute on each side for 4 minutes. Remove from the skillet.
3. In the same skillet, saute the onion and garlic for 5 minutes until the onions begin to brown. Add the crushed tomatoes. Bring to a boil. Lower the heat and let simmer for 5 minutes.
4. Add the turkey, rosemary, thyme, olives, and capers to the skillet. Simmer over low heat for 10 minutes. Add the parsley and serve.

Preparation time: 15 minutes

Stuffed Zucchini Boats

6 servings/serving size: 3–4 oz

This dish is almost as much fun to eat as it is to make.

3 medium zucchini
1 1/2 lb ground turkey breast
1 small onion, minced
1/2 cup finely diced carrot
1/2 cup finely diced red pepper
2 tsp fresh minced basil
1 tsp fresh minced oregano
1 egg, beaten
1 cup store-bought, low-fat, low-sugar
   spaghetti sauce

Very Lean Meat	
Exchange	4
Vegetable Exchange	2
Calories	171
Total Fat	1 g
Saturated Fat	0 g
Calories from Fat	7
Cholesterol	110 mg
Sodium	207 mg
Total Carbohydrate	10 g
Dietary Fiber	2 g
Sugars	6 g
Protein	30 g

Preparation time: 15 minutes

1. Cut each zucchini in half lengthwise and scoop out the inside of each zucchini, leaving a 1-inch shell. Then cut the zucchini boat in half crosswise to make 6 boats. Mince the scooped-out zucchini.
2. Place the hollowed-out zucchini boats in a saucepan and cover with water. Bring water to a boil and boil the boats for 5 minutes. Drain and set aside.
3. In a large skillet, saute the ground turkey until cooked through, about 6 minutes. Remove the turkey from the skillet. Add the onion to the pan drippings and saute for 5 minutes. Add the carrot, red pepper, and reserved minced zucchini. Add the basil and oregano. Add in the ground turkey and egg and mix well.
4. Fill each zucchini boat with the turkey mixture. Place the zucchini boats in a preheated oven at 350 degrees and bake uncovered for 10 minutes. Serve with heated spaghetti sauce drizzled on each zucchini boat (about 2 Tbsp per person).

Lean Beef and Pork

Although it is wise to limit your consumption of high-fat beef, pork, and other cuts of meat, you can still include the lean cuts in a wholesome meal plan. Lean beef is still a wonderful source of protein, zinc, iron, and B vitamins. And pork is leaner than it used to be, thanks to new farm feeding techniques. Try to use the pork tenderloin portion. Just remember to trim the fat carefully off all cuts of meat, and include vegetables and salads with your meal.

French Burgers

Mexican Beef Stir-Fry

Warm Asian Beef Salad

Fiesta Fajitas

Grilled Sirloin with Caper Mustard Sauce

South Sea Island Pork Kabobs

Pork Tenderloin with Country Mustard Cream Sauce

Pork Olé Salad with Roasted Pumpkin Seed Dressing

Good Ol' Pork Barbecue

French Burgers

6 servings/serving size: 3–4 oz

Imagine savoring this juicy burger by the Eiffel Tower!

1 1/2 lb lean ground beef
3 Tbsp Dijon mustard
1 Tbsp minced thyme
1 Tbsp white wine
2 Tbsp minced onion
2 garlic cloves, minced

Medium Fat Meat Exchange	3
Calories	228
Total Fat	15 g
Saturated Fat	6 g
Calories from Fat	136
Cholesterol	70 mg
Sodium	157 mg
Total Carbohydrate	1 g
Dietary Fiber	0 g
Sugars	1 g
Protein	20 g

Combine all ingredients. Shape into 6 patties. Broil until done as desired (3–4 minutes for rare meat, 5–7 minutes for medium meat, and 8–9 minutes for well-done meat).

Preparation time: 8 minutes

Days are like suitcases. By careful arrangement, some people can pack more into them than others.
—Anonymous

Mexican Beef Stir-Fry

6 servings/serving size: 3–4 oz

Although this dish is made in a wok, it has a true southwest flavor.

1 Tbsp canola oil
1 1/2 lb lean sirloin steak, cut into 3-
    inch strips, trimmed of all fat
3 garlic cloves, minced
1 medium onion, minced
1 small red pepper, cut into thin strips
2 tsp chili powder
2 Tbsp lime juice
1 tsp cumin

Lean Meat Exchange	3
Vegetable Exchange	1
Calories	180
Total Fat	7 g
Saturated Fat	2 g
Calories from Fat	67
Cholesterol	65 mg
Sodium	58 mg
Total Carbohydrate	4 g
Dietary Fiber	1 g
Sugars	3 g
Protein	23 g

1. In a wok over medium-high heat, heat the oil. Add the beef and saute until the beef loses its pinkness. Drain any accumulated fat. Remove the beef from the wok.
2. Add the garlic and onions and saute for 5 minutes. Add the red pepper and saute for 5 more minutes.
3. Add the chili powder and lime juice to coat the vegetables. Add the beef back to the skillet and add the cumin. Heat 1 more minute.

Preparation time: 15 minutes

Warm Asian Beef Salad

6 servings/serving size: 3–4 oz

When the cold weather comes, you can still eat a hearty, healthy salad.

Beef:
1 Tbsp peanut oil
1 1/2 lb lean flank steak, cut into
    3-inch strips
2 garlic cloves, minced

Dressing:
1/2 cup rice vinegar
1 Tbsp oyster sauce
1 Tbsp lite soy sauce
1 tsp honey

Salad greens:
6 cups torn romaine lettuce
1/2 cup sliced celery
1/2 cup sliced scallions

Garnish:
1 Tbsp sesame seeds

Lean Meat Exchange	3
Vegetable Exchange	1
Fat Exchange	1/2
Calories	221
Total Fat	11 g
Saturated Fat	4 g
Calories from Fat	102
Cholesterol	54 mg
Sodium	288 mg
Total Carbohydrate	6 g
Dietary Fiber	2 g
Sugars	4 g
Protein	24 g

Preparation time: 10 minutes

1. In a wok over medium-high heat, heat the oil. Add the steak and stir-fry until the steak loses its pinkness. Add the garlic and stir-fry 1 more minute.
2. In a small cup, combine the dressing ingredients. Add to the steak and bring to a boil. Remove the wok from the stove.
3. Combine all the salad ingredients. Place the warm steak mixture on top. Garnish with sesame seeds and serve.

Fiesta Fajitas

6 servings/serving size: 3–4 oz beef and 1/4 cup vegetables in 1 6-inch flour tortilla

Fajitas are fun to eat and make!

1 1/2 lb extra lean ground beef
1 medium onion, diced
2 garlic cloves, minced
1/4 cup each diced red and green
    pepper
1/2 cup corn kernels (fresh or frozen)
1/2 cup diced tomato
3 tsp chili powder
1 tsp cumin
6 6-inch flour tortillas, heated (To
    heat: wrap in foil and place in a 300-
    degree oven until warm and soft, or
    wrap 3 tortillas in 2 damp paper
    towels and microwave on high for 1
    minute.)
1 cup salsa (about 2 Tbsp per serving)

Lean Meat Exchange	3
Starch Exchange	1
Fat Exchange	1 1/2
Vegetable Exchange	1
Calories	347
Total Fat	17 g
Saturated Fat	6 g
Calories from Fat	156
Cholesterol	72 mg
Sodium	258 mg
Total Carbohydrate	23 g
Dietary Fiber	2 g
Sugars	4 g
Protein	25 g

1. In a large skillet over medium-high heat, saute the ground beef until cooked through, about 8 minutes. Drain from skillet, leaving 3 tsp of pan drippings. Set beef aside.
2. In the same skillet, saute the onion, garlic, and peppers for 10 minutes. Add the corn and tomato and cook for 5 more minutes. Add the chili powder and the beef and cook for 1 more minute.
3. Spoon some of the fajita mixture into each warm tortilla. Roll up. Serve each tortilla with 2 Tbsp of salsa.

Preparation time: 10 minutes

Grilled Sirloin with Caper Mustard Sauce

6 servings/serving size: 3–4 oz sirloin with 1–2 Tbsp sauce

This is a delicious main dish with a creamy, mustard-flavored sauce.

Beef:
1 1/2 lb lean sirloin
1 Tbsp coarsely crushed black peppercorns

Sauce:
1/2 cup low-fat mayonnaise
1/4 cup Dijon mustard
1 Tbsp small capers
Fresh ground pepper and salt to taste

Very Lean Meat Exchange	3
Starch Exchange	1/2
Fat Exchange	1/2
Calories	181
Total Fat	7 g
Saturated Fat	2 g
Calories from Fat	60
Cholesterol	65 mg
Sodium	384 mg
Total Carbohydrate	6 g
Dietary Fiber	0 g
Sugars	5 g
Protein	23 g

1. With the heel of your hand, press the peppercorns into the top side of the steak. Grill the sirloin 6 inches from the heat source until done as desired (about 12–13 minutes for rare meat, 15–16 minutes for medium meat, and 18 minutes for well-done meat). Slice into thin slices.
2. Combine all sauce ingredients. Serve steak with mustard sauce.

Preparation time: 6 minutes

South Sea Island Pork Kabobs

6 servings/serving size: 3–4 oz

Ginger and pineapple juice concentrate give this dish a strong fruit flavor.

Pork:
1 1/2 lb lean pork tenderloin, cut into
    2- to 3-inch cubes

Marinade:
2 Tbsp pineapple juice concentrate
1 Tbsp minced ginger
1/3 cup water
2 Tbsp lime juice
2 tsp dark rum

Very Lean Meat	
Exchange	4
Calories	149
Total Fat	4 g
Saturated Fat	1 g
Calories from Fat	37
Cholesterol	66 mg
Sodium	48 mg
Total Carbohydrate	2 g
Dietary Fiber	0 g
Sugars	2 g
Protein	24 g

1. Place the pork cubes in a ziploc bag.
2. Combine all the ingredients for the marinade. Add to the pork. Let the pork marinate for several hours.
3. Thread 6 8- to 10-inch skewers with the marinated pork. Grill 6 inches from the heat source for about 10–15 minutes, rotating the skewers. Make sure the pork is completely cooked through (there should be no traces of pink). Serve over rice if desired.

Preparation time: 8 minutes

Pork Tenderloin with Country Mustard Cream Sauce

6 servings/serving size: 3–4 oz pork with 1/4 cup sauce

Try to use coarse Dijon mustard for special country taste.

2 tsp olive oil
1 1/2 lb pork tenderloin, cut into 3- to
    4-oz fillets
1 cup diced onion
1 12-oz can evaporated skim milk
2 Tbsp coarse Dijon mustard
2 tsp fresh chopped rosemary
2 tsp minced chives
1/4 cup minced parsley
Fresh ground pepper to taste

Very Lean Meat	
Exchange	4
Monounsaturated Fat	
Exchange	1/2
Starch Exchange	1/2
Calories	212
Total Fat	6 g
Saturated Fat	2 g
Calories from Fat	54
Cholesterol	68 mg
Sodium	177 mg
Total Carbohydrate	10 g
Dietary Fiber	1 g
Sugars	7 g
Protein	28 g

1. In a large skillet over medium heat, heat the olive oil. Add the pork slices and saute on each side for 6–7 minutes until no pink remains. Remove the pork from the skillet.
2. In the pan drippings, saute the onion for 10 minutes. Add the evaporated milk, mustard, and rosemary. Bring to a boil, then lower the heat to simmer. Add the pork and simmer for 5 minutes. Add the chives and parsley. Grind in the pepper and simmer for 3 more minutes.

Preparation time: 10 minutes

Pork Olé Salad with Roasted Pumpkin Seed Dressing

6 servings/serving size: 3–4 oz pork and 1/4 cup vegetables

Just add crusty bread to this satisfying summer salad. Since it is sometimes hard to find pumpkin seeds sold in small quantities, buy a larger batch and freeze the remainder to keep it fresh.

Salad:
1 1/2 lb cooked pork tenderloin, sliced
    into 3-inch strips
1/2 cup cooked yellow corn kernels
1 cup diced red pepper
1/2 cup diced red onion
1/2 cup diced jicama (if you can't find
    jicama, you can omit it)
1/2 cup diced tomato
1/4 cup diced mango or papaya

Dressing:
2 Tbsp raw, unsalted pumpkin seeds
6 Tbsp fresh lime juice
2 Tbsp fresh orange juice
2 tsp olive oil
2 Tbsp nonfat sour cream
2 tsp minced cilantro
1 tsp chili powder
Butter lettuce leaves

Lean Meat Exchange	3
Starch Exchange	1/2
Vegetable Exchange	1
Calories	221
Total Fat	8 g
Saturated Fat	2 g
Calories from Fat	71
Cholesterol	66 mg
Sodium	64 mg
Total Carbohydrate	11 g
Dietary Fiber	2 g
Sugars	4 g
Protein	27 g

Preparation time: 20 minutes

1. In a large salad bowl, combine all the salad ingredients.
2. Place the pumpkin seeds in a small dry skillet over medium heat. Toast the seeds until they lightly brown. Remove from the heat.
3. In a blender or food processor, combine the seeds with the juices and oil. Blend 30 seconds. By hand, fold in the sour cream, cilantro, and chili powder. Toss the dressing with the salad and serve on butter lettuce.

Good Ol' Pork Barbecue

6 servings/serving size: 3–4 oz with 1–2 oz bread

This recipe is high in sodium due to the catsup. If you need to reduce sodium in your diet, try using low-sodium catsup.

2 Tbsp canola oil
1 small onion, minced
1 cup catsup
2 Tbsp red wine vinegar
1 Tbsp honey
2 Tbsp Worcestershire sauce
1 cup water
2 tsp paprika
2 tsp chili powder
1/2 tsp cayenne
1 1/2 lb cooked pork tenderloin, shredded or cubed into small pieces
6 slices toasted French, Italian, or multi-grain bread

Lean Meat Exchange	3
Starch Exchange	2
Calories	320
Total Fat	10 g
Saturated Fat	2 g
Calories from Fat	94
Cholesterol	66 mg
Sodium	730 mg
Total Carbohydrate	31 g
Dietary Fiber	3 g
Sugars	10 g
Protein	27 g

Preparation time: 15 minutes

1. To make the sauce, combine all ingredients except the pork and bread in a saucepan. Simmer uncovered over medium heat for 15 minutes until the onion has softened.
2. Prepare the pork and add it to the sauce. Continue to simmer for 5 minutes.
3. Pile the pork filling evenly over each bread slice. Eat with a fork.

Very Quick Vegetables

The phrase "strive for five" is really true when it comes to eating vegetables. Unfortunately, most of the time vegetables just end up as lifeless blobs on our plates. This chapter provides delicious, fast vegetable recipes that everyone will enjoy. You can use either fresh or frozen vegetables, but avoid canned varieties because of the high sodium content and dull flavor.

Although eating fresh vegetables is a tasty part of your healthy lifestyle, avoid the tendency to overbuy them. For the freshest flavor, try to store vegetables for no more than 2 days in your refrigerator. If you want them to last longer, your best bet would be to buy frozen veggies. The new vegetable plastic bags available, with tiny holes to help the vegetables breathe, will keep your vegetables fresher. Look for this in the plastic bag and foil aisle of your grocery store.

For the best nutritional value, try to stick with the vegetable "powerhouses" such as broccoli, cauliflower, carrots, peppers (particularly the red ones), beets, and all the greens, such as mustard, kale, chard, collards, and spinach.

Vegetable Cooking Methods

Carrots with Orange Glaze

Garden-Fresh Green Beans and Tomatoes with Oregano

Asparagus in Brown Sauce

Triple Cabbage Delight

Sesame Kale

Fresh Spinach and Mushroom Medley

Snow Peas with Water Chestnuts and Bamboo Shoots

Baby Red Potatoes with Fresh Herbs

Grilled Summer Squash and Zucchini

Saucy Green Beans and Cauliflower

Vegetable Cooking Methods

Many different techniques are available to cook vegetables. Use methods like the ones below to keep vegetables crisp, colorful, and full of nutrients.

Steaming: This technique requires a little more time than boiling, but preserves levels of some nutrients like Vitamin C, which are diminished by boiling. Steaming helps retain delicate vegetable flavors, and therefore is better suited to mild-tasting vegetables such as summer squash, carrots, and beets, rather than strong-tasting vegetables such as Brussels sprouts and cabbage. For proper steaming, place vegetables on a steamer rack above boiling water in a saucepan. Cover the saucepan tightly to keep in the steam. Replenish the water if you need to during the steaming process. Pasta pots often come with steamer inserts, or use Chinese bamboo steamers that stack and enable you to steam many items at once. Folding steamers fit in most pots.

Stir-frying: This is a very quick method of preparing vegetables. Keep the heat relatively high, and toss the cut vegetables continuously over the heat until they are done, but still slightly crisp. A wok is the best vehicle for stir-frying, but a heavy skillet will do. Make sure your pan is hot enough or the food will absorb too much oil and stick to the sides.

Grilling: This method is suitable for certain vegetables. Sweet peppers, tomatoes, large mushrooms, potatoes, sweet potatoes, and corn are all delicious grilled. Simply brush the vegetables with a little oil to prevent drying and grill. You can place small pieces of vegetables in foil, and then set them on the grill. The rack should be about 6 inches from the heat source and the heat should be about medium.

Microwaving: This technique is best for vegetables you need done in a hurry that normally take a long time to cook. Vegetables are usually microwaved at high power.

Roasting: This is a favorite method of cooking winter squash, potatoes, sweet potatoes, eggplant, peppers, and tomatoes. The dry heat preserves the flavor of these veggies better than steaming. Moisten the vegetable with oil or a marinade and bake in the oven until tender. You can also scatter these vegetables around a chicken or roast to absorb the meat juices as they cook.

Braising: This method cooks vegetables slowly with a small amount of liquid you can then use to make a sauce. The braising liquid is either soup stock or water enhanced for added flavor with onions, garlic, or herbs. The best braising pan is a deep saute pan with a lid; a heavy, wide casserole; or a Dutch oven. Braising is best for slow-cooking vegetables, such as large pieces of carrot, potatoes, or eggplant.

Try experimenting with different herbs and spices. Reaching for the salt shaker all the time limits your culinary imagination (and adds unwanted sodium to your meal plan!). Vegetables have a nice, sweet flavor when cooked properly, so a sprinkle or two of salt is all you really need.

When you just feel like tossing in some herbs for flavor, here are some good matches of vegetables and herbs. Fresh herbs will taste the best. You can use dried herbs, but for best flavor results, make sure they are not more than a year old.

☞ Tarragon for asparagus

☞ Basil for tomatoes, carrots, and potatoes

☞ Thyme for carrots and summer squash

☞ Rosemary for potatoes, peas, and spinach

☞ Mint for peas

☞ Dill for broccoli, corn, and beets

☞ Marjoram for broccoli

Use about 1 Tbsp of chopped herbs for 2 cups of vegetables. Just take a pair of scissors and snip the herb right into the cooked vegetable. Add fresh ground pepper, a dash of olive oil, and serve!

Carrots with Orange Glaze

6 servings/serving size: 1/2 cup

You can also use this glaze for cooked beets.

Carrots:
3 cups diagonally sliced, peeled carrots

Glaze:
1/3 cup fresh orange juice
1/4 cup water
1 Tbsp honey
1 Tbsp fresh lemon juice
1 tsp cinnamon
1/2 tsp nutmeg
1 Tbsp cornstarch or arrowroot
2 Tbsp water

Garnish:
Fresh mint leaves

Vegetable Exchange	2
Calories	54
Total Fat	0 g
Saturated Fat	0 g
Calories from Fat	1
Cholesterol	0 mg
Sodium	48 mg
Total Carbohydrate	13 g
Dietary Fiber	2 g
Sugars	7 g
Protein	1 g

1. Prepare the carrots by steaming them over boiling water on a steamer rack, covered, for 5 minutes. Drain and set aside.
2. In a small saucepan over medium heat, combine the orange juice, water, lemon juice, honey, and spices. Bring to a boil. Reduce the heat and cook for 3 minutes.
3. Combine the cornstarch or arrowroot with the water. Add to the orange juice mixture and cook over low heat until thickened. Pour the orange glaze over the carrots and serve. Garnish with mint leaves.

Garden-Fresh Green Beans and Tomatoes with Oregano

6 servings/serving size: 1/2 cup

Try to purchase vine-ripened tomatoes for this straight-from-the-field side dish.

2 tsp olive oil
1/4 cup diced onion
2 garlic cloves, minced
2 cups cut green beans (trim ends and cut green beans in 1-inch lengths)
1/4 cup low-fat, low-sodium chicken broth
1 medium tomato, diced
1 Tbsp fresh minced oregano
1 Tbsp minced parsley
Fresh ground pepper and salt to taste

Monounsaturated Fat Exchange	1/2
Vegetable Exchange	1
Calories	39
Total Fat	2 g
Saturated Fat	0 g
Calories from Fat	17
Cholesterol	0 mg
Sodium	32 mg
Total Carbohydrate	6 g
Dietary Fiber	2 g
Sugars	2 g
Protein	1 g

1. In a wok or heavy skillet over medium-high heat, heat the oil. Add the onion and garlic and saute for 3 minutes (do not let the garlic brown). Add the green beans and broth, cover, and steam for 3 minutes.
2. Add the diced tomato, cover, and steam 30 seconds. Add the oregano, parsley, pepper, and salt and steam for 30 seconds more. Serve.

Preparation time: 8 minutes

Asparagus in Brown Sauce

6 servings/serving size: 1/2 cup

To prepare asparagus, break off the bottom end and diagonally slice in 1-inch lengths. Choose asparagus that has tightly closed buds and stems that are neither too thin nor too thick. Asparagus is best in the spring.

Asparagus:
2 tsp peanut oil
3 garlic cloves, minced
6 cups sliced asparagus (about 2 lb)

Sauce:
1/2 cup low-fat, low-sodium chicken
   broth
2 Tbsp lite soy sauce
2 Tbsp rice vinegar
1 Tbsp oyster sauce
1 tsp Tabasco sauce
1 tsp sesame oil
1 1/2 Tbsp cornstarch or arrowroot
   powder
3 Tbsp water

Garnish:
1/4 cup minced scallions

Vegetable Exchange	2
Fat Exchange	1/2
Calories	80
Total Fat	3 g
Saturated Fat	1 g
Calories from Fat	27
Cholesterol	0 mg
Sodium	340 mg
Total Carbohydrate	11 g
Dietary Fiber	4 g
Sugars	5 g
Protein	5 g

Preparation time: 8 minutes

1. In a wok over medium-high heat, heat the oil. Add the garlic and saute for 20 seconds. Add the asparagus and stir-fry for 3 minutes.
2. Combine all the sauce ingredients except the cornstarch or arrowroot powder. Add to the asparagus, cover, and steam for 1 minute.
3. Add the cornstarch or arrowroot powder to the water and stir until it is completely dissolved. Add this mixture to the sauce. Cook until sauce is thickened, about 1 minute. Garnish with scallions.

Triple Cabbage Delight

6 servings/serving size: 1/2 cup

Bok choy, green cabbage, and Napa cabbage are delicious with a quick mustard-flavored sauce. Napa cabbage is a large Chinese cabbage with light green leaves. Bok choy cabbage looks a little like celery. To use, cut off the tough base, then slice the stalks, including the leaves. Discard any tough leaves.

Cabbage:
1 cup sliced bok choy cabbage
1 cup sliced green cabbage (1/4 small head)
1 cup sliced Napa cabbage

Sauce:
1/2 cup Dijon mustard
3 Tbsp lite soy sauce
1 tsp sugar
2 Tbsp rice vinegar

Vegetable Exchange	1
Calories	30
Total Fat	1 g
Saturated Fat	0 g
Calories from Fat	8
Cholesterol	0 mg
Sodium	559 mg
Total Carbohydrate	4 g
Dietary Fiber	1 g
Sugars	4 g
Protein	1 g

1. In a large pot of boiling water, add the sliced cabbages and cook for just 1 minute. Drain and splash the cabbage with cold water.
2. Mix all ingredients for the sauce. Add the mustard sauce to the cabbage and toss well. Serve chilled. This dish is good with a fish entree.

Preparation time: 10 minutes

Sesame Kale

6 servings/serving size: 1/2 cup

Kale deserves a wider audience in this country. This vitamin- and fiber-packed vegetable is so easy to prepare.

1 1/2 lb kale
2 tsp sesame oil
2 garlic cloves, minced
1/4 cup low-fat, low-sodium chicken broth
1 Tbsp lite soy sauce
2 tsp toasted sesame seeds
Fresh ground pepper to taste

Vegetable Exchange	1
Fat Exchange	1/2
Calories	52
Total Fat	3 g
Saturated Fat	0 g
Calories from Fat	23
Cholesterol	0 mg
Sodium	127 mg
Total Carbohydrate	6 g
Dietary Fiber	2 g
Sugars	3 g
Protein	2 g

1. Wash the kale, but let the water cling to it. Cut off and discard the tough stems. Slice the leaves once down the middle, then cut them crosswise into 1-inch-wide strips.
2. In a wok, heat the oil. Add the garlic. Saute for 10 seconds. Add the kale and the broth. Cover and steam for 3 minutes until the kale wilts. Add the soy sauce.
3. Top the kale with sesame seeds and fresh ground pepper. Serve.

Preparation time: 8 minutes

Fresh Spinach and Mushroom Medley

6 servings/serving size: 1/2 cup

Popeye was right when he dug into his spinach! Rich in nutrients with a slight peppery flavor, fresh spinach can't be beat.

2 tsp olive oil
2 garlic cloves, minced
1/2 cup canned straw mushrooms, drained (look in the Asian food section of your grocery store, or substitute regular mushrooms)
3/4 lb fresh spinach leaves, washed (do not dry!), stemmed, and coarsely chopped (about 2 1/2 cups)
2 Tbsp fresh lemon juice
Fresh ground pepper and salt to taste

Vegetable Exchange	1
Calories	34
Total Fat	2 g
Saturated Fat	0 g
Calories from Fat	15
Cholesterol	0 mg
Sodium	126 mg
Total Carbohydrate	4 g
Dietary Fiber	2 g
Sugars	1 g
Protein	2 g

1. In a wok or heavy skillet over medium-high heat, heat the oil. Add the garlic and saute for 10 seconds. Add the mushrooms and saute for 2 minutes.
2. Add the spinach, cover, and steam for 2–3 minutes until it wilts. Add the lemon juice and pepper and serve.

Preparation time: 5 minutes

Snow Peas with Water Chestnuts and Bamboo Shoots

6 servings/serving size: 1/2 cup

Snow peas are one of the quickest-cooking vegetables. Be sure to buy only fresh snow peas—anything else pales in comparison!

2 tsp peanut oil
1/2 cup diced onion
1/4 cup diced celery
2 cups trimmed fresh snow peas
1/2 cup sliced water chestnuts
1/2 cup sliced bamboo shoots
1/2 cup low-fat, low-sodium chicken
    broth
Fresh ground pepper and salt to taste

Vegetable Exchange	1
Fat Exchange	1/2
Calories	51
Total Fat	2 g
Saturated Fat	0 g
Calories from Fat	17
Cholesterol	0 mg
Sodium	41 mg
Total Carbohydrate	7 g
Dietary Fiber	2 g
Sugars	4 g
Protein	2 g

1. In a wok over medium-high heat, heat the oil. Add the onion and celery and stir-fry for 3 minutes.
2. Add the snow peas, water chestnuts, bamboo shoots, and broth. Cover and steam 1–2 minutes.
3. Add the pepper and salt to taste. Snow peas should still be crisp and bright green when served.

Preparation time: 10 minutes

Baby Red Potatoes with Fresh Herbs

6 servings/serving size: 1/2 cup

When choosing potatoes for this recipe, seek out very small ones. They will be sweet and moist, and it only takes about 10 minutes for them to boil.

3 cups (about 1 1/2 lb) baby red potatoes, washed and scrubbed (do not peel)
1 Tbsp olive oil
4 garlic cloves, minced
2 tsp minced dill
1 tsp minced mint
1 tsp minced rosemary
Fresh ground pepper to taste

Starch Exchange....	1 1/2
Calories..................	121
Total Fat..................	2 g
Saturated Fat	0 g
Calories from Fat......	22
Cholesterol............	0 mg
Sodium	7 mg
Total Carbohydrate..	23 g
Dietary Fiber............	2 g
Sugars....................	3 g
Protein	2 g

1. In a medium saucepan, cover the potatoes with water and boil for about 10 minutes. Drain and place in a bowl.
2. Toss the potatoes with the remaining ingredients and serve.

Capture time before it flies.
—Anonymous

Grilled Summer Squash and Zucchini

6 servings/serving size: 1/2 small zucchini or squash

Grilling the yellow squash and zucchini is a good way to bring out the flavor.

Squash:
3 small summer squash (combination of zucchini and yellow)

Basting sauce:
1 garlic clove, minced
1/2 tsp paprika
1/2 tsp cumin
2 Tbsp olive oil
1 Tbsp fresh lemon juice

Monounsaturated Fat Exchange	1/2
Vegetable Exchange	1
Calories	29
Total Fat	2 g
Saturated Fat	0 g
Calories from Fat	21
Cholesterol	0 mg
Sodium	1 mg
Total Carbohydrate	2 g
Dietary Fiber	1 g
Sugars	1 g
Protein	0 g

1. Halve each squash, but do not peel. Combine all ingredients for sauce.
2. To grill, place the squash on a rack over medium hot coals with the rack set 6 inches from the heat source. Baste with some of the sauce. Grill the squash about 5 minutes on each side, basting frequently with sauce. Serve.

Preparation time: 7 minutes

Saucy Green Beans and Cauliflower

6 servings/serving size: 1/2 cup

Just a touch of sharp blue cheese makes this dish special!

Vegetables:
1 1/2 cups cauliflower florets
1 1/2 cups trimmed green beans

Sauce:
1 Tbsp low-calorie margarine
1 Tbsp unbleached white flour
1/2 cup evaporated skim milk
1 1/2 oz crumbled blue cheese
2 tsp Dijon mustard

Saturated Fat
   Exchange 1/2
Vegetable Exchange 2
Calories 74
Total Fat .... 3 g
   Saturated Fat .... 2 g
   Calories from Fat 30
Cholesterol .... 6 mg
Sodium .... 164 mg
Total Carbohydrate .... 7 g
   Dietary Fiber .... 2 g
   Sugars .... 3 g
Protein .... 4 g

1. Steam the cauliflower over boiling water on a steamer rack for 5 minutes. Add the green beans and steam for an additional 2–3 minutes. Remove from heat.
2. Meanwhile, make the sauce: in a large skillet, heat the margarine. Add the flour and stir until smooth. Add the milk and cook until bubbly. Add the cheese and mustard. Toss in the cooked vegetables and serve.

Preparation time: 10 minutes

Sweet Endings

Nothing completes a meal like dessert, but who has time to make dessert as well as dinner? Fortunately, preparing dessert does not have to be a complicated process. In this chapter, simple ingredients are turned into spectacular creations.

You'll get the best results with some of the fruit desserts if you use fresh fruit. Canned and frozen fruit does not hold up as well or taste as good. Buying fruits when they are in season will ensure the best-tasting desserts.

So, go ahead—indulge in these healthy sweet endings!

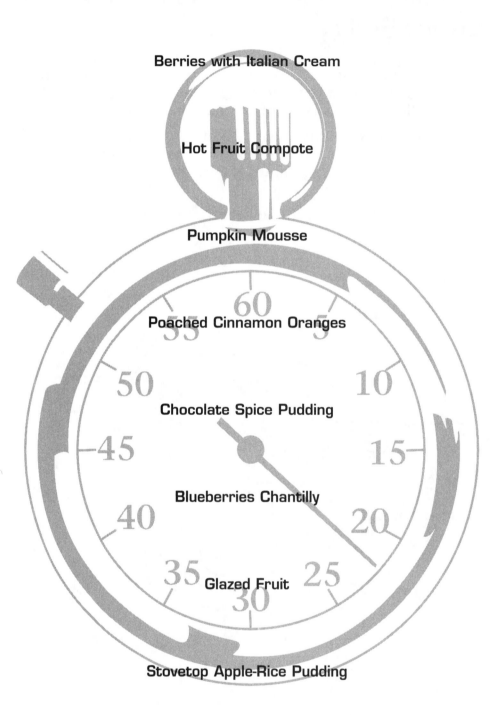

Berries with Italian Cream

Hot Fruit Compote

Pumpkin Mousse

Poached Cinnamon Oranges

Chocolate Spice Pudding

Blueberries Chantilly

Glazed Fruit

Stovetop Apple-Rice Pudding

Berries with Italian Cream

6 servings/serving size: 1/2 cup

This delectable dessert is reminiscent of Italian cannoli, but has much less fat.

3 cups sliced fresh strawberries or
  raspberries
1 tsp sugar
1 15-oz carton part skim ricotta cheese
1 Tbsp Grand Marnier
1 tsp vanilla
1 1/2 tsp grated orange peel

Medium-Fat Meat	
Exchange	1
Fruit Exchange	1
Calories	132
Total Fat	6 g
Saturated Fat	3 g
Calories from Fat	53
Cholesterol	22 mg
Sodium	89 mg
Total Carbohydrate	11 g
Dietary Fiber	2 g
Sugars	7 g
Protein	8 g

1. In a medium bowl, mix together the berries and the sugar. Set aside.
2. With an electric beater, beat together the remaining ingredients until light and fluffy.
3. Divide berries among dessert dishes. Top each serving with a portion of the cream.

Preparation time: 10 minutes

Hot Fruit Compote

6 servings/serving size: 1/2 cup

This dessert will warm you up on a cold winter day!

1 cup diced apples (try Granny Smith
  or Rome)
1/2 cup dried apricots
1/2 cup raisins
1 cup diced pears
1/2 tsp cinnamon
1/4 tsp nutmeg
1/2 cup brandy
2 Tbsp lemon juice
2 tsp honey

Fruit Exchange.......	1 1/2
Calories..................	111
Total Fat...................	0 g
Saturated Fat	0 g
Calories from Fat........	3
Cholesterol.............	0 mg
Sodium	4 mg
Total Carbohydrate..	25 g
Dietary Fiber............	3 g
Sugars..................	19 g
Protein	1 g

Combine all ingredients and mix well.
Place in a casserole dish and bake for 20
minutes until the fruit is soft.

A stitch in time saves nine.
—Anonymous

Pumpkin Mousse

6 servings/serving size: 1/2 cup

Pumpkin is a wonderful source of Vitamin A. Be sure to include this nutritious vegetable in desserts throughout the year, not just during the holidays.

2 cups canned pumpkin (not pumpkin pie filling)
1 Tbsp honey
2 tsp cinnamon
2 tsp grated lemon peel
1 cup part skim ricotta cheese

Starch Exchange	1
Calories	96
Total Fat	3 g
Saturated Fat	2 g
Calories from Fat	31
Cholesterol	13 mg
Sodium	56 mg
Total Carbohydrate	12 g
Dietary Fiber	2 g
Sugars	6 g
Protein	6 g

In a medium bowl, combine the pumpkin, honey, cinnamon, and lemon peel. Mix well. Fold in the ricotta cheese. Refrigerate for 1 hour and serve.

Preparation time: 6 minutes

Poached Cinnamon Oranges

6 servings/serving size: 1/2 cup

Jazz up plain citrus with a warm cinnamon syrup. (If you use unsweetened grape juice, the nutrient analysis in parentheses after the red wine analysis applies.)

3 large oranges, peeled and sliced into 1/2-inch rounds
2 cups red wine or unsweetened grape juice
1 Tbsp honey
2 cinnamon sticks
2 tsp grated orange peel
2 tsp vanilla

Fruit Exchange	1 (2)
Calories	83 (111)
Total Fat	0 g (0 g)
Saturated Fat	0 g (0 g)
Calories from Fat	1 (2)
Cholesterol	0 g (0 g)
Sodium	2 mg (3 mg)
Total Carbohydrate	16 g (28 g)
Dietary Fiber	2 g (3 g)
Sugars	12 g (24 g)
Protein	1 g (1 g)

1. Prepare the oranges and set aside.
2. In a medium saucepan over medium heat, combine the wine or juice, honey, and cinnamon sticks. Bring to a boil. Reduce the heat and cook for 15 minutes.
3. Remove from the heat and add the vanilla and orange peel. Pour over the oranges in a bowl and refrigerate 1 hour. Serve.

Preparation time: 10 minutes

Chocolate Spice Pudding

6 servings/serving size: 1/2 cup

Chocolate lovers, rejoice! This spicy pudding tastes like the pudding of your childhood (but it's a much healthier version).

1/3 cup unsweetened cocoa powder
1/4 cup sugar
1 Tbsp cornstarch or arrowroot powder
1/2 tsp ginger
1/4 tsp allspice
1 tsp cinnamon
3 cups evaporated skim milk
1 egg yolk, slightly beaten
3 tsp vanilla

Skim Milk Exchange	1
Other Carbohydrate Exchange	1
Calories	157
Total Fat	2 g
Saturated Fat	1 g
Calories from Fat	16
Cholesterol	40 mg
Sodium	149 mg
Total Carbohydrate	27 g
Dietary Fiber	1 g
Sugars	20 g
Protein	11 g

1. Mix first 6 ingredients in a saucepan. Stir in the milk and egg yolk. Cook until the mixture thickens, stirring constantly.
2. Remove from heat and add vanilla. Pour into 6 custard dishes. Chill and serve.

Preparation time: 10 minutes

Blueberries Chantilly

6 servings/serving size: 1/2 cup fruit with 1/4 cup topping

Clouds of light sour cream and cream cheese surround plump, juicy blueberries.

2 cups fresh blueberries
1 cup fresh raspberries
1 cup low-fat sour cream
1/2 cup low-fat cream cheese
1 Tbsp orange juice
1 Tbsp honey
1 tsp cinnamon
2 tsp orange peel

Saturated Fat Exchange	1 1/2
Fruit Exchange	1
Calories	136
Total Fat	7 g
Saturated Fat	5 g
Calories from Fat	67
Cholesterol	27 mg
Sodium	94 mg
Total Carbohydrate	15 g
Dietary Fiber	3 g
Sugars	10 g
Protein	3 g

Place the blueberries and raspberries in a large bowl. With electric beaters, whip together the sour cream, cream cheese, orange juice, honey, and cinnamon until light and fluffy. Spread over the top of the berries. Garnish with orange peel and serve.

Preparation time: 10 minutes

Glazed Fruit

6 servings/serving size: 1/2 cup

This jewel-colored compote is almost too pretty to eat.

1 cup fresh blueberries
1 cup sliced strawberries
1 cup sliced peaches
1/4 cup low-sugar blackberry preserves
1/4 cup low-sugar orange marmalade
2 Tbsp lemon juice
1 tsp grated lemon peel

Fruit Exchange	1
Calories	58
Total Fat	0 g
Saturated Fat	0 g
Calories from Fat	2
Cholesterol	0 mg
Sodium	12 mg
Total Carbohydrate	14 g
Dietary Fiber	2 g
Sugars	8 g
Protein	0 g

1. Grouping together in rows, place the fruit in a large glass bowl.
2. In two separate small saucepans, heat each jam with one half of the lemon juice and lemon peel until it boils.
3. Pour each melted jam on one half of the fruit. Serve.

Preparation time: 8 minutes

Stovetop Apple-Rice Pudding

6 servings/serving size: 1/2 cup

Apple pie spice and applesauce make this a delicious variation of traditional rice pudding.

Pudding:
2 cups evaporated skim milk
1 8-oz jar unsweetened applesauce
1/2 cup raisins
2 Tbsp fructose
1 tsp apple pie spice
1 1/2 cups quick-cooking rice

Garnish:
Apple pie spice

Starch Exchange....	1 1/2
Fruit Exchange	1
Skim Milk Exchange...	1/2
Calories...................	222
Total Fat..................	0 g
Saturated Fat	0 g
Calories from Fat	3
Cholesterol............	3 mg
Sodium	102 mg
Total Carbohydrate..	46 g
Dietary Fiber...........	1 g
Sugars.................	22 g
Protein	9 g

1. In a saucepan, combine the milk, applesauce, raisins, fructose, and apple pie spice. Bring to a boil, then stir in the rice.
2. Cover and simmer for about 10–15 minutes until liquid is absorbed. Spoon into dessert dishes and dust with apple pie spice. Serve warm or cold.

Preparation time: 6 minutes

Complete Menus for Every Day and Entertaining

When you need a complete menu in a hurry, look no further than these appetizing theme menus—suitable for every day and for entertaining. All menus serve 6 people. Shopping lists are provided, as well as a "countdown" timetable telling you the order of food preparation steps so all parts of your meal will be ready at the same time!

Romantic Dining

On Valentine's Day or any other special occasion, light the candles, set out the china, and enjoy this meal.

Menu

Broiled Salmon with Roasted Red Pepper Sauce
Herbed Potatoes
Green Beans with Shiitake Mushrooms
Fresh Raspberries

Shopping List

1 1/2 lb salmon fillets
Olive oil
Lemon juice
1 12-oz jar roasted red
  peppers
Evaporated skim milk
Dried or fresh oregano
Onions

1 1/2 lb small red potatoes
1 lb fresh green beans
1/2 lb fresh shiitake
  mushrooms
Lite soy sauce
Low-fat, low-sodium chicken
  broth
1 1/2 pints raspberries

Broiled Salmon with Roasted Red Pepper Sauce

6 servings/serving size: 3 oz salmon with 2–3 Tbsp sauce

Salmon:
1 1/2 lb salmon fillets
2 tsp olive oil
2 Tbsp fresh lemon juice

Sauce:
2 tsp olive oil
1 medium onion, minced
1 12-oz jar roasted red peppers,
   drained and chopped
3 Tbsp evaporated skim milk
2 tsp fresh minced oregano (or 1 tsp
   dried)
Fresh ground pepper and salt to taste

Monounsaturated Fat Exchange	1
Lean Meat Exchange	3
Vegetable Exchange	1
Calories	240
Total Fat	13 g
Saturated Fat	2 g
Calories from Fat	116
Cholesterol	77 mg
Sodium	168 mg
Total Carbohydrate	5 g
Dietary Fiber	1 g
Sugars	3 g
Protein	25 g

1. Combine the lemon juice and olive oil and brush over the salmon. Let the salmon sit at room temperature for 10 minutes.
2. To make the sauce, heat the oil in a small skillet over medium-high heat. Add the onion and saute for 5 minutes.
3. In a blender, puree the onions with the roasted red peppers. Add the evaporated milk and oregano. Season with pepper and mix well.
4. Place the salmon on a broiler rack set 6 inches from the heat source. Broil the salmon for about 10 minutes until the salmon is tender.
5. Heat the sauce in a small saucepan. To serve, place a small pool of sauce on a dinner plate. Top with a 3-oz salmon fillet. Spoon some sauce on top. Repeat with all fillets.

Preparation time: 15 minutes

Herbed Potatoes

6 servings/serving size: 1/2 cup

1 1/2 lb small red potatoes
1 1/2 tsp olive oil
6 sprigs rosemary
6 sprigs thyme
2 Tbsp white wine
2 1/2 tsp paprika

Starch Exchange....	1 1/2
Calories..................	110
Total Fat..................	1 g
Saturated Fat	0 g
Calories from Fat	11
Cholesterol.............	0 mg
Sodium	6 mg
Total Carbohydrate..	23 g
Dietary Fiber............	2 g
Sugars...................	2 g
Protein	2 g

1. Preheat the oven to 400 degrees. Wash and scrub the potatoes. Cut each potato in half.
2. Place about 1/2 cup of potatoes on 6 squares of foil large enough to fold over. Divide the olive oil, herbs, wine, and paprika evenly over each packet. Seal the packets and place in the oven.
3. Bake for 30 minutes. Let cool for 5 minutes. Place a packet on each plate and let each person carefully open the packet.

Preparation time: 10 minutes

Green Beans with Shiitake Mushrooms

6 servings/serving size: 1/2 cup

3 Tbsp low-fat, low-sodium chicken broth
1 small shallot, minced
1 lb trimmed green beans, cut into 1-inch lengths
1/2 lb sliced and stemmed shiitake mushrooms
2 Tbsp lite soy sauce

Vegetable Exchange	2
Calories	41
Total Fat	0 g
Saturated Fat	0 g
Calories from Fat	3
Cholesterol	0 mg
Sodium	208 mg
Total Carbohydrate	9 g
Dietary Fiber	3 g
Sugars	4 g
Protein	2 g

1. In a skillet over medium heat, heat the broth. Add the shallots and saute for 3 minutes.
2. Add the green beans and shiitake mushrooms. Stir-fry for 5 minutes. Add the soy sauce. Cover and steam for 2 minutes.

Preparation time: 8 minutes

Countdown

1. Prepare the Herb Potatoes.

2. While the Herb Potatoes are baking, prepare the Roasted Red Pepper Sauce. Set sauce aside in a saucepot.

3. Wash the raspberries, place in individual glass dessert dishes, and place the dishes in the refrigerator.

4. Prepare the salmon, but do not broil yet.

5. Prepare the Green Beans with Shiitake Mushrooms.

6. Remove the potatoes from the oven. Place the salmon steaks under the broiler.

7. Heat the Roasted Red Pepper Sauce.

8. Place the salmon, green beans, and potatoes on a plate and serve.

9. Serve fresh raspberries for dessert!

Well-arranged time is the surest mark
of a well-arranged mind.
—Pitman

Lazy Sunday Brunch

Brunch is a wonderful way to entertain, and a casual, fun way to start the day.

Menu

Scrambled Eggs in Crisp Potato Skins
Spicy Turkey Sausages
Whole Grain Toast
Banana Mint Slushes

Shopping List

Eggs or egg substitutes
3 large baking potatoes
Olive oil
Paprika
1 red pepper
1 green pepper
Low-fat or nonfat cream
  cheese
Cilantro

Parsley
Dried oregano
Cumin
Cloves
1 lb lean ground turkey
Whole grain bread
3 bananas
Mint
Nonfat milk

Scrambled Eggs in Crisp Potato Skins

6 servings/serving size: 2 eggs with 1/2 large baked potato skin

This is a creative way to serve an old favorite!

Eggs:
Nonstick cooking spray
1/2 cup each diced red and green pepper
12 egg substitutes, beaten
2 Tbsp low-fat or nonfat cream cheese

Shells:
3 large cooked baking potatoes, cut in half and scooped out (leave a 1-inch shell)
1 1/2 tsp olive oil
Paprika

Very Lean Meat Exchange	2
Starch Exchange	1
Calories	153
Total Fat	2 g
Saturated Fat	1 g
Calories from Fat	18
Cholesterol	3 mg
Sodium	241 mg
Total Carbohydrate	18 g
Dietary Fiber	1 g
Sugars	3 g
Protein	15 g

1. Preheat the oven to 400 degrees. Place the scooped-out potato skins on a baking sheet. Brush the skins with oil. Dust each shell with paprika. Bake in the oven for 20 minutes.
2. To prepare the eggs, place a nonstick skillet over medium heat and spray the skillet lightly with cooking spray. Add the peppers and saute for 5 minutes.
3. Add the eggs and cook about 5 minutes until eggs are set. Add the cream cheese and blend in well.
4. To serve, pile the eggs into the potato shells and dust tops with more paprika.

Preparation time: 10 minutes

Spicy Turkey Sausages

6 servings/serving size: 2 oz

1/2 cup finely minced cilantro
1/2 cup finely minced parsley
2 tsp fennel seeds
1/4 tsp cumin
1/4 tsp cloves
1 tsp crushed red pepper flakes
Fresh ground pepper and salt to taste
1 lb lean ground turkey (your butcher
    can grind this for you)

Very Lean Meat	
Exchange	2
Calories	84
Total Fat	0 g
Saturated Fat	0 g
Calories from Fat	4
Cholesterol	50 mg
Sodium	58 mg
Total Carbohydrate	0 g
Dietary Fiber	0 g
Sugars	0 g
Protein	18 g

1. Combine all ingredients in a food processor, or mix together very well by hand.
2. Let the turkey mixture chill for several hours. Then form the mixture into patties.
3. In a nonstick skillet, cook the patties on each side for 3–4 minutes until the turkey is cooked through.

Preparation time: 5 minutes

Banana Mint Slushes

6 servings/serving size: 1/2 cup

2 bananas
10 mint leaves
2 tsp vanilla extract
3 cups skim milk
1 cup ice cubes

Fruit Exchange	1/2
Skim Milk Exchange	1/2
Calories	76
Total Fat	0 g
Saturated Fat	0 g
Calories from Fat	3
Cholesterol	2 mg
Sodium	63 mg
Total Carbohydrate	14 g
Dietary Fiber	1 g
Sugars	11 g
Protein	5 g

Place the bananas in a blender and puree. Add the remaining ingredients and blend well. Serve from a tall pitcher in frosty glasses.

Preparation time: 5 minutes

Countdown

1. Prepare the turkey sausage mixture the night before to let flavors blend.
2. The next day, prepare the potato skins.
3. Slice the whole-grain bread, if not already sliced.
4. Cook the sausages and keep warm.
5. Cook the eggs and place in the cooked potato shells.
6. While toasting whole-grain bread, prepare the banana mint slushes.
7. Place the eggs, sausages, and bread on plates. Pour the slushes in a pitcher. Serve.

Time stays long enough for anyone who will use it.
—Leonardo da Vinci

Country French Dinner

The French have an undeniable flair for beautiful food presentation and wonderful gastronomic experiences. Your friends will think you studied at the finest Paris cooking school when you serve them this delicious meal!

Menu

Chicken with Tarragon and Mushrooms
Carrots with Fennel
Roasted Potatoes
Macedoine of Fruit

Shopping List

3 whole chicken breasts
Tarragon
1 lb white mushrooms
White wine
4 shallots
1 lb small carrots
Port wine

Fennel seeds
Olive oil
1 lb small red potatoes
2 apples
2 bananas
Red grapes
2 oranges

Chicken with Tarragon and Mushrooms

6 servings/serving size: 3–4 oz chicken with sauce

3 whole chicken breasts, halved,
   boned, and skinned
6 sprigs tarragon
3 shallots, minced
1/4 cup dry white wine
1 lb sliced mushrooms
Fresh ground pepper and salt to taste

Very Lean Meat	
Exchange	4
Vegetable Exchange	1
Calories	163
Total Fat	3 g
Saturated Fat	1 g
Calories from Fat	30
Cholesterol	73 mg
Sodium	89 mg
Total Carbohydrate	4 g
Dietary Fiber	1 g
Sugars	1 g
Protein	28 g

1. Preheat the oven to 350 degrees. Tear aluminum foil into 6 squares large enough to seal the chicken.
2. Place a chicken breast on each foil piece. Place the remaining ingredients on top of each breast, dividing evenly. Fold the foil over to seal. Place the chicken packets in the oven and bake for about 15 minutes.
3. Place the packets on individual plates and let each person carefully open the packet.

Preparation time: 10 minutes

Carrots with Fennel

6 servings/serving size: 1/2 cup

3 cups baby carrots
3 Tbsp port wine
1 Tbsp fennel seeds
1 Tbsp olive oil
Fresh ground pepper and salt to taste

Monounsaturated Fat
    Exchange 1/2
Vegetable Exchange....... 2
Calories 60
Total Fat .... 2 g
    Saturated Fat .... 0 g
    Calories from Fat 22
Cholesterol .... 0 mg
Sodium .... 72 mg
Total Carbohydrate .... 8 g
    Dietary Fiber .... 3 g
    Sugars .... 3 g
Protein .... 1 g

1. Preheat the oven to 350 degrees. Tear aluminum foil into 6 pieces large enough to seal the carrots.
2. Divide all ingredients evenly among all 6 pieces of foil. Crimp to seal. Place the packets in the oven and bake for 15 minutes, until carrots are tender.
3. Place the packets on individual plates and let each person carefully open the packet.

Preparation time: 8 minutes

Macedoine of Fruit

6 servings/serving size: 1/2 cup

2 medium apples, unpeeled and thinly
  sliced
2 bananas, thinly sliced
1 cup red grapes
1 orange, peeled and sliced
1 Tbsp orange liqueur
2 Tbsp lemon juice

Fruit Exchange	1 1/2
Calories	102
Total Fat	1 g
Saturated Fat	0 g
Calories from Fat	5
Cholesterol	0 mg
Sodium	2 mg
Total Carbohydrate	25 g
Dietary Fiber	3 g
Sugars	19 g
Protein	1 g

Combine all ingredients in a large glass
bowl. Toss to mix well. Refrigerate and
serve chilled.

Preparation time: 10 minutes

Countdown

1. Prepare the Macedoine of Fruit and set in the refrigerator until dessert time.

2. Drizzle red potatoes with a little olive oil and place in the oven to roast for 30 minutes.

3. Prepare the carrots.

4. Prepare the chicken.

5. Remove the potatoes from the oven and place on plates with the chicken and carrot packets.

6. Serve dessert.

There are only twenty-four hours in a day.
—Proverb

Warm Summer Evening

Dine under the stars with this easy summer meal.

Menu

Crab Louis
Peppers Vinaigrette
Crusty Rolls
Grilled Glazed Peaches

Shopping List

1 1/2 lb lump crabmeat
Low-fat mayonnaise
Evaporated skim milk
Chili sauce
Tabasco sauce
Green pepper
Scallions
Romaine lettuce
1 each red, yellow, and green
    peppers

Red wine vinegar
Fresh chives
Garlic
Olive oil
Whole grain rolls
3 large peaches
Low-calorie margarine
Orange juice

Crab Louis

6 servings/serving size: 3 oz

1 1/2 lb lump crabmeat
1/2 cup low-fat mayonnaise
2 Tbsp evaporated skim milk
2 Tbsp chili sauce
1 Tbsp lemon juice
2 Tbsp diced green pepper
3 Tbsp minced scallions
Romaine lettuce leaves

Very Lean Meat Exchange	3
Starch Exchange	1/2
Calories	143
Total Fat	3 g
Saturated Fat	0 g
Calories from Fat	27
Cholesterol	96 mg
Sodium	529 mg
Total Carbohydrate	8 g
Dietary Fiber	0 g
Sugars	5 g
Protein	20 g

Combine all ingredients. Set crabmeat on top of romaine lettuce leaves and serve.

Preparation time: 10 minutes

Peppers Vinaigrette

6 servings/serving size: 1/2 cup

1 each small green, yellow, and red
   peppers, thinly sliced
2 Tbsp olive oil
1/4 cup red wine vinegar
1 tsp sugar
2 Tbsp minced chives
Fresh ground pepper and salt to taste

Monounsaturated Fat Exchange	1
Vegetable Exchange	1
Calories	60
Total Fat	5 g
Saturated Fat	1 g
Calories from Fat	41
Cholesterol	0 mg
Sodium	25 mg
Total Carbohydrate	5 g
Dietary Fiber	1 g
Sugars	3 g
Protein	1 g

1. In a pot of boiling water, add the peppers and cook for 2 minutes. Drain and plunge in ice water. Drain again.
2. In a blender, blend together the remaining ingredients. Pour over the peppers and mix well. Serve.

Preparation time: 15 minutes

Grilled Glazed Peaches

6 servings/serving size: 1/2 large peach

3 large peaches, pitted and halved, unpeeled
1/4 cup low-calorie margarine
2 Tbsp orange juice

Fruit Exchange	1/2
Fat Exchange	1/2
Calories	59
Total Fat	3 g
Saturated Fat	0 g
Calories from Fat	23
Cholesterol	0 mg
Sodium	41 mg
Total Carbohydrate	9 g
Dietary Fiber	2 g
Sugars	7 g
Protein	1 g

1. Prepare a hot grill. In a separate pan, melt the margarine and orange juice until syrupy.
2. Place the peaches, cut side down, on an oiled rack 6 inches from the heat source. Brush the syrup over the peaches. Grill the peaches about 10 minutes, turning and basting frequently, until the peaches are hot and glazed. Remove from the grill and serve.

Preparation time: 5 minutes

Countdown

1. Prepare the peppers and chill.

2. Prepare the Crab Louis and place on a platter.

3. Set out the rolls.

4. Remove the peppers from the refrigerator and serve with the Crab Louis and rolls.

5. Grill the peaches and eat.

To choose time is to save time.
—Francis Bacon

Dinner Italiano

Menu

Chicken Rigatoni
Oven-Baked Parmesan Zucchini
Tossed Salad with Balsamic Vinaigrette
Layered Vanilla Yogurt Parfaits

Shopping List

1 lb rigatoni
3/4 lb chicken breasts
1 onion
1 green pepper
1 15-oz jar marinara sauce
Small zucchini
Parmesan cheese
6 cups salad greens
3 cups plain nonfat yogurt
1 banana
1 cup green grapes
1 cup strawberries
Grapenuts™ cereal

Eggs or egg substitute
Unbleached white flour
Olive oil
Balsamic vinegar
Vanilla
Dried basil
Dried oregano
Garlic powder
Paprika
Dijon mustard
Fresh garlic
Shallots
Fructose

Chicken Rigatoni

6 servings/serving size: 2 oz chicken with 1 cup pasta

1 Tbsp olive oil
12 oz boneless, skinless chicken
    breasts, cubed
1 medium onion, chopped
1 green pepper, seeded, cored, and cut
    into matchstick strips
1 15-oz jar marinara sauce
Fresh ground pepper to taste
6 cups cooked rigatoni pasta

Lean Meat Exchange	2
Vegetable Exchange	2
Calories	312
Total Fat	7 g
Saturated Fat	2 g
Calories from Fat	62
Cholesterol	35 mg
Sodium	284 mg
Total Carbohydrate	41 g
Dietary Fiber	4 g
Sugars	6 g
Protein	19 g

1. To prepare the sauce, heat the oil in a large skillet over medium heat. Add the chicken and saute until chicken is no longer pink. Remove from the skillet.
2. In the remaining pan juices, saute the onion and pepper. Add the cooked chicken to the skillet and add the marinara sauce. Grind in pepper.
3. Let the sauce simmer for about 5 minutes. Pour over the rigatoni and serve.

Preparation time: 15 minutes

Oven-Baked Parmesan Zucchini

6 servings/serving size: 1/2 cup

4 small zucchini, scrubbed and
diagonally sliced about 1/2 inch
thick
2 eggs or egg substitutes, beaten
2 Tbsp unbleached white flour
3 Tbsp Parmesan cheese
1 tsp dried oregano
1/2 tsp dried basil
1 tsp paprika
1/2 tsp garlic powder
1 Tbsp olive oil

Monounsaturated Fat Exchange	1/2
Vegetable Exchange	1
Calories	51
Total Fat	3 g
Saturated Fat	1 g
Calories from Fat	25
Cholesterol	1 mg
Sodium	57 mg
Total Carbohydrate	4 g
Dietary Fiber	1 g
Sugars	2 g
Protein	3 g

1. Preheat the oven to 350 degrees. Dip each zucchini slice into the beaten egg.
2. In a large ziploc bag, combine the remaining ingredients except the oil. Shake the mixture well. Add the zucchini slices and shake well.
3. Place the zucchini slices on a nonstick cookie sheet. Drizzle the zucchini slices with the olive oil.
4. Bake for 7–8 minutes until zucchini is golden brown.

Preparation time: 10 minutes

Balsamic Vinaigrette

8 servings/serving size: 2 Tbsp

1/2 cup balsamic vinegar
2 tsp minced garlic
3 tsp Dijon mustard
1 Tbsp olive oil
1/4 cup minced shallots
Fresh ground pepper and salt to taste

Monounsaturated Fat Exchange	1/2
Calories	23
Total Fat	2 g
Saturated Fat	0 g
Calories from Fat	16
Cholesterol	0 mg
Sodium	42 mg
Total Carbohydrate	2 g
Dietary Fiber	0 g
Sugars	1 g
Protein	0 g

In a small bowl, whisk together all ingredients. Serve over salad greens. You can store this dressing in the refrigerator for 2 weeks.

Preparation time: 5 minutes

Layered Vanilla Yogurt Parfaits

6 servings/serving size: 1/2 cup yogurt with 1/2 cup fruit

3 cups plain nonfat yogurt
2 tsp vanilla extract
3 tsp fructose
1 banana, sliced
1 cup halved green grapes
1 cup sliced strawberries
1/4 cup Grapenuts™ cereal

Fruit Exchange	1
Skim Milk Exchange	1/2
Calories	126
Total Fat	0 g
Saturated Fat	0 g
Calories from Fat	3
Cholesterol	3 mg
Sodium	129 mg
Total Carbohydrate	25 g
Dietary Fiber	2 g
Sugars	19 g
Protein	8 g

1. In a small bowl, combine the yogurt, vanilla, and fructose. Place a bottom layer of the yogurt mixture in parfait, wine, or champagne glasses.
3. In another bowl, combine the fruits. Add a layer of fruit on top of the yogurt. Continue layering the yogurt and fruit until each glass has three layers, ending with yogurt.
4. Top each parfait with a sprinkle of Grapenuts™ cereal. Chill until ready to serve.

Preparation time: 10 minutes

Countdown

1. Prepare the Layered Vanilla Yogurt Parfaits and refrigerate until dessert time.

2. Prepare the salad dressing. Refrigerate.

3. Wash the salad greens. Place in a salad bowl. Cover and refrigerate.

4. Slice the zucchini. Coat with the Parmesan mixture and place on a cookie sheet. Place the cookie sheet in the refrigerator and let the coating adhere to the zucchini for 15 minutes before baking.

5. Prepare the dessert and refrigerate.

6. Boil the rigatoni.

7. Prepare the sauce for the rigatoni.

8. Place the zucchini in the oven and bake for 7 minutes.

9. Pour sauce over pasta and place in serving bowl.

10. Take zucchini out of the oven and place in serving bowl.

11. Shake dressing, pour over greens, and toss.

12. Serve dinner.

13. Serve dessert.

Method will teach you to win time.
—Goethe

Appendix: Nutrition Analyses for Quick Fixes

Salsa Salad
Starch Exchange—1
Vegetable Exchange—1
Calories—94
Total Fat—0 g
  Saturated Fat—0 g
  Calories from Fat—3
Cholesterol—0 mg
Sodium—102 mg
Total Carbohydrate—19 g
  Dietary Fiber—5 g
  Sugars—3 g
Protein—5 g

Bean Spread
Starch Exchange—1/2
Calories—38
Total Fat—1 g
  Saturated Fat—0 g
  Calories from Fat—5
Cholesterol—6 mg
Sodium—62 mg
Total Carbohydrate—5 g
  Dietary Fiber—1 g
  Sugars—1 g
Protein—4 g

Zippy Pasta
Starch Exchange—3
Calories—253
Total Fat—3 g
  Saturated Fat—0 g
  Calories from Fat—27
Cholesterol—1 mg

Sodium—160 mg
Total Carbohydrate—46 g
  Dietary Fiber—6 g
  Sugars—4 g
Protein—10 g

Navy Bean Soup
Starch Exchange—1/2
Vegetable Exchange—2
Calories—169
Total Fat—1 g
  Saturated Fat—0 g
  Calories from Fat—10
Cholesterol—0 mg
Sodium—484 mg
Total Carbohydrate—33 g
  Dietary Fiber—7 g
  Sugars—9 g
Protein—8 g

Quick Refried Beans
Monounsaturated Fat
  Exchange—1/2
Starch Exchange—1
Calories—98
Total Fat—3 g
  Saturated Fat—0 g
  Calories from Fat—26
Cholesterol—0 mg
Sodium—105 mg
Total Carbohydrate—14 g
  Dietary Fiber—4 g
  Sugars—3 g
Protein—5 g

Turkey Ball Soup
Very Lean Meat
  Exchange—3
Starch Exchange—1/2
Calories—148
Total Fat—3 g
  Saturated Fat—1 g
  Calories from Fat—25
Cholesterol—86 mg
Sodium—172 mg
Total Carbohydrate—9 g
  Dietary Fiber—0 g
  Sugars—1 g
Protein—22 g

Clear Asian Soup
Starch Exchange—1 1/2
Calories—112
Total Fat—2 g
  Saturated Fat—0 g
  Calories from Fat—14
Cholesterol—0 mg
Sodium—280 mg
Total Carbohydrate—21 g
  Dietary Fiber—2 g
  Sugars—3 g
Protein—5 g

Rice and Pea Soup
Starch Exchange—2
Calories—144
Total Fat—3 g
  Saturated Fat—1 g
  Calories from Fat—24

Cholesterol—1 mg
Sodium—109 mg
Total Carbohydrate—27 g
Dietary Fiber—3 g
Sugars—2 g
Protein—6 g

Tasty Pasta Soup
Very Lean Meat
Exchange—1
Starch Exchange—1 1/2
Calories—162
Total Fat—4 g
Saturated Fat—1 g
Calories from Fat—34
Cholesterol—21 mg
Sodium—92 mg
Total Carbohydrate—22 g
Dietary Fiber—1 g
Sugars—2 g
Protein—12 g

Fast Onion Soup
Monounsaturated Fat
Exchange—1
Starch Exchange—1
Vegetable Exchange—1
Calories—149
Total Fat—6 g
Saturated Fat—1 g
Calories from Fat—50
Cholesterol—1 mg
Sodium—244 mg
Total Carbohydrate—2 g
Dietary Fiber—2 g
Sugars—7 g
Protein—6 g

Pasta Pie
Starch Exchange—3
Calories—239
Total Fat—4 g
Saturated Fat—1 g
Calories from Fat—33
Cholesterol—1 mg
Sodium—40 mg
Total Carbohydrate—42 g
Dietary Fiber—4 g
Sugars—3 g
Protein—9 g

Artichoke Pasta Salad
Starch Exchange—3
Vegetable Exchange—1
Calories—265
Total Fat—2 g
Saturated Fat—0 g
Calories from Fat—20
Cholesterol—0 mg
Sodium—415 mg
Total Carbohydrate—50 g
Dietary Fiber—4 g
Sugars—7 g
Protein—9 g

Sesame Noodles
Starch Exchange—3
Fat Exchange—1/2
Calories—261
Total Fat—5 g
Saturated Fat—1 g
Calories from Fat—49
Cholesterol—53 mg
Sodium—25 mg
Total Carbohydrate—44 g

Dietary Fiber—3 g
Sugars—4 g
Protein—9 g

Hungarian Noodles
Starch Exchange—3
Saturated Fat
Exchange—1/2
Calories—267
Total Fat—6 g
Saturated Fat—3 g
Calories from Fat—51
Cholesterol—66 mg
Sodium—46 mg
Total Carbohydrate—45 g
Dietary Fiber—3 g
Sugars—5 g
Protein—9 g

Fast Mediterranean Meal
Starch Exchange—3 1/2
Calories—285
Total Fat—4 g
Saturated Fat—1 g
Calories from Fat—35
Cholesterol—1 mg
Sodium—78 mg
Total Carbohydrate—52 g
Dietary Fiber—4 g
Sugars—4 g
Protein—11 g

Cool Salad
Starch Exchange—1 1/2
Fruit Exchange—1
Saturated Fat
Exchange—1/2

Calories—190
Total Fat—4 g
  Saturated Fat—2 g
  Calories from Fat—37
Cholesterol—13 mg
Sodium—19 mg
Total Carbohydrate—35 g
  Dietary Fiber—2 g
  Sugars—10 g
Protein—3 g

Viva Mexicana
Starch Exchange—2 1/2
Calories—197
Total Fat—3 g
  Saturated Fat—0 g
  Calories from Fat—25
Cholesterol—0 mg
Sodium—90 mg
Total Carbohydrate—36 g
  Dietary Fiber—4 g
  Sugars—3 g
Protein—7 g

Down By the Bay
Very Lean Meat Exchange—1
Starch Exchange—1 1/2
Calories—169
Total Fat—2 g
  Saturated Fat—0 g
  Calories from Fat—22
Cholesterol—57 mg
Sodium—87 mg
Total Carbohydrate—25 g
  Dietary Fiber—1 g
  Sugars—1 g
Protein—11 g

Fast Fried Rice
Starch Exchange—2
Calories—145
Total Fat—2 g
  Saturated Fat—0 g
  Calories from Fat—16
Cholesterol—0 mg
Sodium—425 mg
Total Carbohydrate—28 g
  Dietary Fiber—2 g
  Sugars—3 g
Protein—4 g

Rice Crust Pizza
Lean Meat Exchange—1
Starch Exchange—1 1/2
Vegetable Exchange—1
Calories—202
Total Fat—4 g
  Saturated Fat—2 g
  Calories from Fat—38
Cholesterol—47 mg
Sodium—476 mg
Total Carbohydrate—29 g
  Dietary Fiber—1 g
  Sugars—3 g
Protein—10 g

Tuna Pate
Very Lean Meat
  Exchange—2
Calories—61
Total Fat—1 g
  Saturated Fat—0 g
  Calories from Fat—5
Cholesterol—10 mg
Sodium—315 mg

Total Carbohydrate—1 g
  Dietary Fiber—0 g
  Sugars—1 g
Protein—12 g

Salmon Nicoise
Lean Meat Exchange—2
Vegetable Exchange—2
Calories—161
Total Fat—6 g
  Saturated Fat—1 g
  Calories from Fat—57
Cholesterol—31 mg
Sodium—648 mg
Total Carbohydrate—8 g
  Dietary Fiber—3 g
  Sugars—4 g
Protein—18 g

Tonnato Sauce
Very Lean Meat
  Exchange—1
Vegetable Exchange—2
Calories—90
Total Fat—2 g
  Saturated Fat—0 g
  Calories from Fat—17
Cholesterol—8 mg
Sodium—321 mg
Total Carbohydrate—9 g
  Dietary Fiber—2 g
  Sugars—5 g
Protein—9 g

Couscous Tuna Salad
Very Lean Meat Exchange—1
Starch Exchange—2

Calories—179
Total Fat—3 g
  Saturated Fat—0 g
  Calories from Fat—24
Cholesterol—8 mg
Sodium—98 mg
Total Carbohydrate—27 g
  Dietary Fiber—2 g
  Sugars—1 g
Protein—11 g

Quick Salmon Burgers

Very Lean Meat
  Exchange—3
Fat Exchange—1/2
Calories—137
Total Fat—5 g
  Saturated Fat—1 g
  Calories from Fat—48
Cholesterol—65 mg
Sodium—482 mg
Total Carbohydrate—3 g
  Dietary Fiber—0 g
  Sugars—1 g
Protein—18 g

Index

Alphabetical List of Recipes

Angel Hair Pasta with Tomato Seafood Cream Sauce 62
Arugula and Watercress Salad 43
Asian Tuna Steaks..80
Asparagus in Brown Sauce 119
Baby Red Potatoes with Fresh Herbs..124
Balsamic Vinaigrette...161
Banana Mint Slushes..146
Berries with Italian Cream 129
Black Bean Hummus 21
Blueberries Chantilly...134
Bombay Chicken 94
Broccoli Salad 47
Broiled Crab Cakes...72
Broiled Salmon with Roasted Red Pepper Sauce 139
Canned Bean Quick Fixes 11
Canned Broth Quick Fixes 12
Canned Fish Quick Fixes..16
Carrots with Fennel...150
Carrots with Orange Glaze..117
Chicken and Grapes..93
Chicken Marsala..96
Chicken Paprikash...95
Chicken Rigatoni...159
Chicken Stir-Fry with Vegetables...87
Chicken Tarragon Salad 92
Chicken with Tarragon and Mushrooms...149
Chocolate Spice Pudding 133
Cod and Shrimp Soup...39
Coriander Carrot Salad..50
Couscous Tabouli 64
Crab Louis 154
Creamy Corn Chowder..32
Creamy Pumpkin Soup 36
Crunchy Chicken with Asparagus 88
Curried Chicken Salad with Grapes..91
Fiesta Fajitas...106
French Burgers..103
Fresh Beet and Carrot Salad 46
Fresh Snow Pea and Tri-Colored Pepper Salad 52
Fresh Spinach and Mushroom Medley..122

Fresh Tomato Bruschetta...26
Garden-Fresh Green Beans and Tomatoes with Oregano 118
Ginger and Lime Salmon 78
Glazed Fruit 135
Golden Butternut Squash Soup 37
Good Ol' Pork Barbecue...111
Green Beans with Shiitake Mushrooms...141
Grilled Glazed Peaches..156
Grilled Salmon with Rice Vinegar Splash 75
Grilled Sirloin with Caper Mustard Sauce 107
Grilled Summer Squash and Zucchini..125
Grilled Turkey with Garlic Sauce 98
Halibut in Foil 77
Healthy Coleslaw..48
Herbed Potatoes..140
Hot and Sour Soup 38
Hot Fruit Compote 130
Indian Rice Curry...66
Italian Bean Salad..51
Layered Vanilla Yogurt Parfaits 162
Low-Fat Dijon Potato Salad..49
Macedoine of Fruit 151
Mediterranean Seafood Pasta 79
Mexican Beef Stir-Fry 104
Moroccan Couscous with Chickpeas..63
Oriental Ginger Pork..28
Oven-Baked Parmesan Zucchini 160
Pasta Puttanesca 59
Pasta Quick Fixes...13
Peppers Vinaigrette..155
Poached Cinnamon Oranges 132
Pork Olé Salad with Roasted Pumpkin Seed Dressing...................110
Pork Tenderloin with Country Mustard Cream Sauce 109
Pumpkin Mousse...131
Quick Chili 34
Red Pepper Hummus...20
Rice Quick Fixes 15
Rigatoni with Eggplant and Mushrooms..60
Roasted Potatoes..152
Roasted Red Pepper Soup 31
Saucy Green Beans and Cauliflower 126
Scrambled Eggs in Crisp Potato Skins..144
Sesame Basil Chicken Tidbits...25
Sesame Kale 121

Sesame Noodles...58
Shells Agli Olio..61
Shrimp Fra Diablo..76
Sliced Tomatoes with Italian Parsley Dressing...............................53
Snow Peas with Water Chestnuts and Bamboo Shoots....................123
South Sea Island Pork Kabobs...108
South-of-The-Border Chicken with Variations................................83
Southwestern Chicken Salad..90
Speedy Black Bean Soup..33
Spiced Scallops..27
Spicy Chicken with Peppers...89
Spicy Hummus..19
Spicy Turkey Sausages...145
Spinach Dip..23
Spinach Orange Salad..45
Steamed Oriental Sole..74
Stovetop Apple-Rice Pudding..136
Stuffed Zucchini Boats...100
Sun-Dried Tomato and Basil Dip...22
Swordfish with Fresh Tomato Sauce..71
Tandoori Shrimp...73
Triple Cabbage Delight...120
Turkey Burritos...97
Turkey Provençal..99
Tuscan Bean Soup..35
Two-Tone Rice Pilaf...67
Vegetable Cooking Methods...115
Vegetable Rice and Beans...65
Walnut-Flavored Artichoke and Grapefruit Salad...........................44
Warm Asian Beef Salad..105
White Bean Pate...24
"Wok" This Way...86

Subject Index

Appetizer Recipes...17

Asian Food
    Asian Tuna Steaks...80
    Chicken Stir-Fry with Vegetables...87
    Hot and Sour Soup...38
    Oriental Ginger Pork..28
    Sesame Noodles...58

Asian Food—*continued*
　　Snow Peas with Water Chestnuts and Bamboo Shoots 123
　　Warm Asian Beef Salad 105

Beans
　　Black Bean Hummus...21
　　Canned Bean Quick Fixes..11
　　Italian Bean Salad..51
　　Quick Chili...34
　　Speedy Black Bean Soup 33
　　Tuscan Bean Soup 35
　　Vegetable Rice and Beans..65
　　White Bean Pate...24

Beef Recipes...101

Chicken (see *Poultry*)

Couscous
　　Couscous Tabouli 64
　　Moroccan Couscous with Chickpeas...63

Dessert Recipes...127

Dips (see *Hummus*)
　　Spinach...23
　　Sun-Dried Tomato and Basil 22

Fruit
　　Banana Mint Slushes..146
　　Berries with Italian Cream 129
　　Blueberries Chantilly 134
　　Glazed Fruit..135
　　Grilled Glazed Peaches...156
　　Hot Fruit Compote..130
　　Macedoine of Fruit..151
　　Poached Cinnamon Oranges...132
　　Stovetop Apple-Rice Pudding 136

Hummus
　　Black Bean 21
　　Red Pepper...20
　　Spicy 19

Marinade, Variations for Chicken 84

Pasta
Angel Hair Pasta with Tomato Seafood Cream Sauce 62
Chicken Rigatoni 159
Mediterranean Seafood Pasta...79
Pasta Puttanesca...59
Quick Fixes...13
Rigatoni with Eggplant and Mushrooms 60
Sesame Noodles..58
Shells Agli Olio...61

Pate, White Bean 24

Pork
Good Ol' Pork Barbecue...111
Oriental Ginger Pork..28
Pork Olé Salad with Roasted Pumpkin Seed Dressing........................110
Pork Tenderloin with Country Mustard Cream Sauce.........................109
South Sea Island Pork Kabobs..108

Potatoes
Baby Red Potatoes with Fresh Herbs 124
Herbed Potatoes 140
Low-Fat Dijon Potato Salad 49
Roasted Potatoes 152

Poultry (see *Turkey*)
Chicken Rigatoni 159
Chicken with Tarragon and Mushrooms 149
Recipes..81
Sesame Basil Chicken Tidbits...25

Pumpkin
Creamy Pumpkin Soup...36
Pumpkin Mousse..131

Rice
Indian Rice Curry...66
Quick Fixes...15
Stovetop Apple-Rice Pudding 136
Two-Tone Rice Pilaf...67
Vegetable Rice and Beans..65

Salad Recipes 41

Salmon
Broiled Salmon with Roasted Red Pepper Sauce 139
Ginger and Lime Salmon...78
Grilled Salmon with Rice Vinegar Splash.................................75

Seafood
Angel Hair Pasta with Tomato Seafood Cream Sauce 62
Cod and Shrimp Soup...39
Crab Louis 154
Recipes..69
Spiced Scallops 27

Shrimp
Cod and Shrimp Soup...39
Shrimp Fra Diablo..76
Tandoori Shrimp 73

Soup Recipes...29

Tomatoes
Angel Hair Pasta with Tomato Seafood Cream Sauce 62
Fresh Tomato Bruschetta 26
Garden-Fresh Green Beans and Tomatoes with Oregano.....118
Sliced Tomatoes with Italian Parsley Dressing 53
Sun-Dried Tomato and Basil Dip..22
Swordfish with Fresh Tomato Sauce...71

Turkey
Grilled Turkey with Garlic Sauce...98
Spicy Turkey Sausages 145
Stuffed Zucchini Boats 100
Turkey Burritos..97
Turkey Provençal...99

Vegetable Recipes...113

Vegetarian Recipes..55

About the Author

Robyn Webb has made her mark in the field of nutrition. In addition to her well-known Virginia nutritional practice, consisting of counseling services, low-fat catering, a low-fat cooking school, and lecture services, she is also the successful author of *A Pinch of Thyme: Easy Lessons for a Leaner Life* (Kendall/Hunt Publishing, 1994). She is also the author of the *Flavorful Seasons Cookbook* (American Diabetes Association).

Webb specializes in providing fast and easy ways for people to maintain their health. Recipes developed by Webb are designed with the busy person in mind. Most take less than an hour to prepare and are simple to follow. The results are delicious.

Her expertise and eye-opening ideas have been well-noted by the media. Webb has been featured in articles in *Woman's Day, Cosmopolitan, USA Today, The Associated Press, Virginia Business Magazine, Washingtonian, The Washington Business Journal,* and the *Washington Post.* Webb has appeared nationally on CBS News with Dan Rather, on ESPN with fitness expert Denise Austin, on The TV Food Network, on the QVC home shopping network, and on Working Woman. Her local Washington, D.C., credits include Broadcast House Live, WJLA Channel 7, News Channel 8, and WRC-TV's "Fighting Fat" series. Webb has also been a guest on several radio talk shows. She is also the 1995 Virginia recipient of the National Healthy American Fitness Leader award by the President's Council on Fitness and Exercise.

Webb's career spans twelve years. She received her Master of Science degree in nutrition from Florida State University. Her work with the American Diabetes Association includes the taste analysis for five cookbooks in the *Healthy Selects* series and taste analysis for *Forecast* magazine recipes. Webb grew up in a family challenged by diabetes and is well-versed in the need for careful meal planning and food preparation.

New Books from the American Diabetes Association Library of Cooking and Self-Care

Flavorful Seasons Cookbook

More than 400 unforgettable recipes that combine great taste with all the good-for-you benefits of a well-balanced meal. Warm up winter with recipes for Christmas, New Year's, St. Patrick's Day, and others. Welcome spring with recipes for Good Friday, Palm Sunday, Easter, Memorial Day, more. Cool off those hot summer days with fresh recipes for the Fourth of July, family barbecues, Labor Day, others. When fall chills the air you'll be ready with recipes for Halloween, Thanksgiving, and more. #4613-01
Nonmember: $16.95; ADA Member: $13.55

Diabetes Meal Planning Made Easy

The new Food Guide Pyramid helps make nutritious meal planning easier than ever. This new guide simplifies the concept by translating diabetes food guidelines into today's food choices. Simple, easy-to-follow chapters will help you understand the new food pyramid; learn all about the six food groups and how to incorporate them into a healthy diet; make smart choices when it comes to sweets, fats, and dairy products; shop smart at the grocery store; make all your meals easier by planning ahead; more. #4706-01
Nonmember: $14.95; ADA Member: $11.95

Magic Menus for People With Diabetes

Mealtime discipline can be a major struggle—calculating exchanges, counting calories, and figuring fats is complicated and time-consuming. But now you have more than 200 low-fat, calorie-controlled selections—for breakfast, lunch, dinner, and snacks—to automatically turn the struggle into a smorgasbord. Choose from Chicken Cacciatore, Veal Piccata, Chop Suey, Beef Stroganoff, Vegetable Lasagna, plus dozens more. But don't worry about calculating all your nutrients—it's done for you *automatically.* #4707-01
Nonmember: $14.95; ADA Member: $11.95

World-Class Diabetic Cooking

Travel around the world at every meal with a collection of 200 exciting new low-fat, low-calorie recipes. Features Tai, Caribbean, Scandinavian, Italian, Greek, Spanish, Chinese, Japanese, African, Mexican, Portuguese, German, and Middle Eastern recipes. All major food categories—appetizers, soups, salads, pastas, meats, breads, and desserts—are highlighted. Includes a nutrient analysis and exchanges (conveniently converted to US exchanges) for each recipe. #4617-01
Nonmember: $11.95; ADA Member: $9.55

Southern-Style Diabetic Cooking

Dig into a savory collection of southern-style recipes *without* guilt. *Southern-Style Diabetic Cooking* takes traditional Southern dishes and turns them into great-tasting but good-for-you recipes. Features more than 100 selections, including appetizers, soups, salads, breads, main dishes, vegetables, side dishes, and desserts. Complete nutrient analysis with each recipe. Suggestions on appropriate frequency of serving and ways to fit special treats or holiday menus into a meal plan. #4615-01
Nonmember: $11.95; ADA Member: $9.55

American Diabetes Association Complete Guide to Diabetes

Finally, *all* areas of diabetes self-care are covered in the pages of *one* book. Whether you have type 1 or type 2 diabetes, you'll learn all about symptoms and causes, diagnosis and treatment, handling emergencies, complications and prevention, achieving good blood sugar control, and more. You'll also discover advice on nutrition, exercise, sex, pregnancy, travel, family life, coping, and health insurance. 464 pages. Conveniently indexed for quick reference to any topic. Hdcover, #4808-01   Pbk, #4809-01
Nonmember: $19.95; ADA Member: $17.95

101 Tips for Staying Healthy With Diabetes (and Avoiding Complications)

Developing complications of diabetes is a constant threat without proper self-care. *101 Tips for Staying Healthy* offers the inside track on the latest tips, techniques, and strategies for preventing and treating complications. You'll find simple, practical suggestions for avoiding complications through close blood-sugar control, plus easy-to-follow treatment strategies for slowing and even halting the progression of existing complications. Helpful illustrations with each tip. #4810-01
Nonmember: $12.50; ADA Member: $9.95

101 Tips for Improving Your Blood Sugar

Keeping your blood sugar near normal not only makes you feel better, it also reduces the risk of developing diabetes-related complications, such as nerve, eye, and kidney disease. No matter where you are, no matter what you're doing, *101 Tips* will help you stay in control. Tips cover diet, exercise, travel, weight loss, insulin injection and rotation, illness, sex, and much more. Now it's a snap to learn all about blood sugar, what affects it, and everything you can do to control it. #4805-01
Nonmember: $12.50; ADA Member: $9.95

Order Toll-Free! 1-800-ADA-ORDER
VISA • Mastercard • American Express

Or send your check or money order to:
American Diabetes Association
ATTN: Order Fulfillment Department
P.O. Box 930850
Atlanta, GA 33193-0850

Shipping & Handling:
up to $25.....................add $4.99
$25.01–$60..................add $5.99
above $60........add 10% of order

Allow 2–3 weeks for shipment. Add $4.99 to shipping & handling for each extra shipping address. Add $15 for each overseas shipment. Prices subject to change without notice.

Also available in bookstores nationwide